## MAIMONIDES ON THE ORIGIN OF THE WORLD

Although Maimonides' discussion of creation is one of his greatest contributions – he himself claimed that belief in creation is second in importance only to belief in God – there is still considerable debate on what that contribution was. Kenneth Seeskin takes a close look at the problems Maimonides faced and the sources from which he drew. He argues that Maimonides meant exactly what he said: the world was created by a free act of God, so the existence of everything other than God is contingent. In religious terms, existence is a gift. To reach this conclusion, Seeskin examines Maimonides' view of God, miracles, the limits of human knowledge, and the claims of astronomy to be a science. Clearly written and closely argued, *Maimonides on the Origin of the World* takes up questions of perennial interest.

Kenneth Seeskin, a Professor of Philosophy at Northwestern University and winner of the Koret Jewish Book Award (2001), is the author of *Jewish Philosophy in a Secular Age, Maimonides: A Guide for Today's Perplexed, No Other Gods: the Modern Struggle against Idolatry, Searching for a Distant God: The Legacy of Maimonides,* and *Autonomy in Jewish Philosophy.* He is also the editor of the forthcoming book, *The Cambridge Companion to Maimonides.*

# Maimonides on the Origin of the World

KENNETH SEESKIN
*Northwestern University*

CAMBRIDGE
UNIVERSITY PRESS

CAMBRIDGE UNIVERSITY PRESS
Cambridge, New York, Melbourne, Madrid, Cape Town, Singapore, São Paulo

Cambridge University Press
40 West 20th Street, New York, NY 10011-4211, USA

www.cambridge.org
Information on this title: www.cambridge.org/9780521845533

First published 2005

Printed in the United States of America

*A catalog record for this publication is available from the British Library.*

*Library of Congress Cataloging in Publication Data*
Seeskin, Kenneth, 1947–
Maimonides on the origin of the world / Kenneth Seeskin.
p.   cm.
Includes bibliographical references and index.
ISBN 0-521-84553-X (hardback)
1. Maimonides, Moses, 1135–1204 – Views on creation.   2. Creation.
3. Bible. O. T. Genesis I – Criticism, interpretation, etc., Jewish.   4. Philosophy,
Ancient.   5. Philosophy, Medieval.   6. Philosophy, Jewish.   I. Title.
B759.M34S44   2005
213′.092 – dc22         2004020299

ISBN-13   978-0-521-84553-3 hardback
ISBN-10   0-521-84553-X hardback

*To*

*Ethelyne Wasserman*

# Contents

# Abbreviations

| | |
|---|---|
| *CCP* | *The Cambridge Companion to Plotinus*, edited by Lloyd P. Gerson |
| *EN* | Plotinus, *The Enneads* |
| *GP* | Maimonides, *Guide of the Perplexed* |
| *M* | *Maimonides: A Collection of Critical Essays*, edited by Joseph A. Buijs |
| *MP* | *Maimonides and Philosophy*, edited by S. Pines and Y. Yovel |
| *MS* | *Maimonidean Studies*, edited by Arthur Hyman |
| *MT* | Maimonides, *Mishneh Torah* |
| *OTW* | *On the eternity of the world [by] St. Thomas Aquinas, Siger of Brabant [and] St. Bonaventure*, translated by C. Vollert, L. H. Kendzierski, and P. M. Byrne |
| *PEC* | Herbert Davidson, *Proofs for Eternity, Creation, and the Existence of God in Medieval Islamic and Jewish Philosophy* |
| *PSO* | Edward Grant, *Planets, Stars, and Orbs: The Medieval Cosmos* |
| *PM* | *Perspectives on Maimonides*, edited by Joel Kraemer |
| *SFDG* | Kenneth Seeskin, *Searching for a Distant God* |
| *SHPR* | Harry A. Wolfson, *Studies in the History and Philosophy of Religion* |
| *ST* | Thomas Aquinas, *Summa Theologiae* |
| *TCC* | Richard Sorabji, *Time, Creation, and the Continuum* |
| *WL* | Gersonides, *Wars of the Lord* |

# Introduction

To ask about the origin of the world is to ask why there is something rather than nothing. Although this question may seem like a natural one to us, it would be a mistake to assume that everyone regarded it so. Aristotle did not ask it, and there is serious doubt whether Plato did. Their concern was with the structure of the world, not its origin. Although Plotinus argued that all things have a common source in the first principle, he is thinking about the eternal procession of the world, a process that does not take place in time and is governed by metaphysical necessity. The first suggestion that the existence of the world is contingent and results from the free choice of God occurs in Genesis 1. I say *suggestion* because the text takes the form of a narrative rather than a philosophic argument and is subject to various interpretations.

In the Middle Ages, the question of origin became central because it was closely linked to questions about God. If the world is not eternal but was brought into existence, it is reasonable to conclude that there was an agent responsible for its coming to be and that this agent can act in a spontaneous fashion. Put otherwise, it is reasonable to conclude that the world is the product of God's will. If, on the other hand, the world has always existed, then even though God may be responsible for its existence, God cannot act in a spontaneous fashion, which is to say that God must always be doing the same thing. Although some thinkers ascribed will to the second conception of God, Maimonides protests that a God who cannot do anything different is ruled by necessity and cannot have a will as we normally understand the term. In addition to bringing the world into existence, the first conception of God also allows for miracles, revelation, and redemption; the second does not. So the question of origin was not just historical but, in an important way, theological as well. How one understands the origin of the world has a direct bearing on what one takes the world to be. What one takes the world to be has a direct bearing on what one takes God to be.

Although it is generally recognized that Maimonides' treatment of the question of origin is one of his major contributions to philosophy, there is little agreement about what that contribution was. According to one view, he defended what he took to be the position of the Torah and one of the pillars of the Law: the world was brought into existence out of nothing in the first instant of time. In short, time and motion were created together. I refer to this as creation *ex nihilo* and *de novo*. According to those who stress the esoteric nature of the *Guide of the Perplexed*, Maimonides says he accepts the position of the Torah so as not to offend traditional readers. But the truth is he is committed to an eternal world that proceeds from God by necessity, the world as described by the science of his day. According to a third view, he is committed to a compromise view similar to that described in Plato's *Timaeus*: the world was created in the first instant of time out of preexistent matter. If the structure of the world is imposed *de novo*, its material component is eternal.

All three views can be reconciled with Genesis 1, but it is clear that they have very different implications. Without as much as the possibility of miracles, revelation, or redemption, the biblical text would have to undergo a radical reinterpretation – so radical that one might well ask what of the biblical worldview remains. If the world were created from preexistent matter, one might well ask what the status of this matter is. Does it exist independently of God? Does it impose any limitations on God? Or is it created by God prior to the imposition of order and structure? Beyond these questions is the fact that Maimonides takes the Platonic theory of creation to imply that if the world came into existence, at some point it will perish. If so, what happens to the claim that God is a faithful and steadfast ruler? And what happens to claims of eternal life or promises of salvation?

As I read Maimonides, the Torah view is right not only because it allows us to retain substantial portions of the biblical worldview but because it rests on a superior philosophic foundation. The problem with the other two views is that they assume the creation of the world resembles the origin of a particular thing within it: that it requires the imposition of form on matter as prescribed by Aristotelian natural science. Why, asks Maimonides, should we assume this is so? If God does not resemble a human being, why should we assume divine production must resemble animal or vegetable production? There are good reasons to trust natural science when it comes to things we can observe. But why should we trust it when it comes to God? Why can divine production not proceed in a wholly different fashion, so that the origin of the world would not be anything like the fertilization of an egg or the growth of a plant from a seed?

The fact that Maimonides casts doubt on a naturalistic view of creation does not mean that he distrusted natural science altogether. On the contrary, he is convinced it is correct if we limit its application to the earthly realm. He begins to have doubts when we get to astronomy, pointing out that although Ptolemy's calculations are much more accurate than Aristotle's, Aristotle's theory of motion makes more sense. Finally, he has considerable doubt when we get to God and the origin of the world. To cast doubt on something is not to prove that the opposite view is correct. Despite his preference for the Torah view, Maimonides continues to say that the other views are possible and that the question of how the world came to be is not susceptible to demonstration. Rather than a subtle hint that he wants to distance himself from the Torah view, these remarks should be interpreted as no more than an honest assessment of the epistemological predicament in which Maimonides found himself: although the question of origin is important, the limits of human knowledge prevent us from resolving it with complete certainty.

What, then, is Maimonides' contribution? In addition to pointing out the limits of natural science and defending the biblical worldview, he called attention to a fundamental feature of human existence: the world does not present itself to us as the effect of an eternal process that can only culminate in one result, but as the object of a free and benevolent will. Thus, the world is contingent in the sense that God could have created a different world or no world at all. In a world of this sort, there are limits to what the human mind can understand and no point in trying to go beyond them. In a word, existence is a gift. It is given to us by God and could be taken away just as easily. The proper stance for a person who understands this is not intellectual complacency but humility and gratitude. That is what enables Maimonides to say that, along with monotheism, belief in creation is one of the pillars of the Law.

## Introduction

There are several people whose intelligence, patience, and words of encouragement helped to make this book possible: Cristina D'Ancona Costa, Lenn Goodman, Menachem Kellner, Tzvi Langermann, David Novak, Norbert Samuelson, and Josef Stern. I also thank Herbert Davidson, Seymour Feldman, Arthur Hyman, Alfred Ivry, and Richard Sorabji for books and articles that enabled me to go deeper into this issue than I ever thought I could.

# 1

# God and the Problem of Origin

L ET ME BEGIN IN A GENERAL WAY BY TALKING ABOUT monotheism. As has been pointed out many times, monotheism is more than a numerical claim about God. In addition to asserting that there is only one God, it holds that this God is in some sense unique. Thus, Maimonides (*GP* 1.57, p. 133) maintains that to say that God is one is to say that God has no equal. We can understand "no equal" in either of two ways. The first is to follow the *via negativa* and argue that God bears no resemblance to anything else. God is neither a body, nor a force in a body, nor anything that resembles them. The second is to say that God exists necessarily and that everything else is dependent on God. In the beginning of the *Mishneh Torah*, Maimonides makes this point by saying that all beings other than God need God so that none would exist if God did not.[1]

By the time he gets to the *Guide of the Perplexed,* Maimonides argues that the existence of a God with no equal and the creation of the world are the two pillars on which monotheism rests.[2] According to *GP* 3.29 (p. 516), both were espoused by Abraham:[3]

> However, when the pillar of the world grew up and it became clear to him that there is a separate deity that is neither a body nor a force in a body and that all the stars and the spheres were made by Him, and he understood that the fables upon which he was brought up were absurd, he began to refute their doctrine and to show up their opinions as false; he publicly manifested his disagreement with them and called in the name of the Lord, God of the world – both of the existence of the deity and the creation of the world in time by that deity being comprised in that call.

There is no need to spend a great deal of time on Maimonides' negative theology. If there is no likeness between God and anything else, the difference between God and other things is not one of degree but of kind. Thus (*GP* 1.35, p. 80): "Everything that can be ascribed to God . . . differs in every respect from our attributes, so that no definition can comprehend the one thing and the other." In another passage (*GP* 1.56, pp. 130–31), he goes so far as to say that words such as *knowledge, power,* and *will* are completely equivocal when used of us and God, and thus it is not true that God's knowledge and power are greater than ours, God's will more universal than ours, or God's existence more permanent than ours. It is not true because to say that it is would imply that there is a common measure of comparison and thus some degree of similarity.

---

[1] *MT* 1, Basic Principles of the Torah, 1.3.

[2] In addition to *GP* 2.25, see 2.13, p. 282; 2.27, p. 332; 3.50, p. 613.

[3] The same sentiment is expressed at *GP* 2.13, p. 282, and 3.50, p. 613.

A mustard grain, in Maimonides' opinion, has more in common with the outermost sphere of the world than we do with God.

So rigorous is Maimonides on this point that he denies there can be any sort of relation between God and other things. Following Aristotle, Maimonides understands relation in terms of reciprocity: if $x$ is the father of $y$, by that very fact, $y$ is the son of $x$.[4] A relation, then, is a bridge, an attribute that inheres in two substances at once and joins one to the other. If this is so, relation can only join things that resemble each other in some respect. Maimonides (*GP* 1.52, p. 118) makes this point by saying that only things in the same species can stand in relation to one another. To use his example, one finite intellect can be greater than another, and one color darker than another, but there is no possibility of a relation between the intellect and color because they have nothing in common, nor between a hundred cubits and the heat of a pepper, nor clemency and bitterness.

It follows that there is no possibility of a relation between a necessary being and a contingent one, for if there were, there would be an attribute that inheres in God and links the divine essence to something else. This would mean that God is affected by and in some sense dependent on a part of creation. Just as a father's nature is changed and partially determined by the relation to his son, God would be changed and partially determined by His relation to the world. Maimonides wants us to see that as soon as we begin to talk this way, we compromise God's simplicity and treat God like an ordinary object of experience.

The problem is that as we normally understand it, causality is a relation. Commenting on Aristotle, Maimonides writes (*GP* 2.22, p. 317): "There subsists necessarily a certain conformity between the cause and its effect."[5] Behind this remark is the view that when

---

[4] See Aristotle, *Categories* 7.3.
[5] Cf. Aquinas, *ST* 1.4.2.

two things interact with each other, an attribute that is present in one comes to be present in the other, as when fire passes heat to an iron bar. For Aristotle the effect is potentially what the cause is actually, from which it follows that when it becomes actual, the effect must resemble the cause.[6] This is exactly what Maimonides claims does not obtain between God and the world, because in his view, there is absolutely no resemblance between them. The world is spatial and temporal; God is outside space and time altogether. The world is complex; God is simple. How, then, can God be responsible for the motion of a body like a heavenly sphere?

Although he did not embrace negative theology, Aristotle faced the same problem. How can God be responsible for the motion of the first heaven if God is not subject to change? According to W. D. Ross, Aristotle's God is an efficient cause by virtue of being the final cause.[7] In other words, God causes the motion of the first heaven not by imparting a force that gets it moving but by being the object of desire.[8] To use Aristotle's own analogy, it is like a person we dislike who touches us without our touching him.[9]

It may be objected that Aristotle never attributes efficient causality to the Prime Mover and that efficient causality cannot be reduced to final causality without doing serious damage to our understanding of what it means to be a cause.[10] Suppose that an intelligent being represents divine perfection to itself. As Maimonides indicates (GP 2.4, p. 256), an idea of divine perfection, although necessary for efficient causality, is not sufficient because nothing will happen unless there is desire for it. But even desire is

---

[6] Aristotle, De Anima 417a18–20.

[7] See W. D. Ross, Aristotle: Metaphysics, pp. cxxxiii–cxxiv.

[8] Aristotle, Metaphysics 1072a26–27. Note, however, that there is at least one place where Aristotle describes the causality of the Prime Mover in physical terms: Physics 267b6–9. According to Ross (ibid.), this is "an incautious expression which should not be pressed."

[9] Aristotle, On Generation and Corruption 323a25–33.

[10] For the case against ascribing efficient causality to the Prime Mover, see Joseph Owens, The Doctrine of Being in the Aristotelian Metaphysics, pp. 443, 468.

not sufficient. To borrow an example from Marvin Fox, a person suffering from paralysis may have an intense desire for an object, but without the ability to apply force, there still will not be motion.[11] The problem is that God cannot apply physical force to anything. As Maimonides (ibid.) recognizes, to say that God causes the movement of the first heaven is really to say that the first heaven desires to be like God. If so, it is the desire of the first heaven that is responsible for movement and is the true efficient cause.

In his commentary on the *Timaeus,* Proclus argues that if the Prime Mover is responsible for the motion of the heavenly bodies, then by parity of reason, he must also be responsible for their existence.[12] No doubt this is an attempt to say that the Prime Mover should have been more like Plato's Demiurge. To understand this criticism, consider the outline of Aristotle's account of the Prime Mover. It is impossible for there to be an infinite body. No finite body can contain more than finite power.[13] A finite power can only account for motion over a finite period of time. But the motion of the heavenly bodies is eternal. Therefore, there must be a separate cause of that motion that is not a finite body.

The question that Proclus raises is this: why should the same argument not work for existence? If no body contains more than a finite power, it can only account for existence over a finite period of time. The heavenly bodies exist eternally. Therefore, there must be a separate cause of their existence that is not a body. Although this is a reasonable inference, there is no evidence that Aristotle drew it. For Aristotle, efficient causality tells us how one existent

---

[11] Marvin Fox, *Interpreting Maimonides,* p. 232.

[12] See Proclus, *Commentary on the Timaeus* (Diehl, Vol. 1, pp. 266–67); cf. *Elements of Theology,* prop. 12. For further discussion of this point, see Davidson, *PEC,* pp. 281–82.

[13] Aristotle, *Physics* 266b25–26. For further discussion, see Davidson, "The Principle That a Finite Body Can Contain Only Finite Power," *Studies in Jewish Religious and Intellectual History,* ed. S. Stein and R. Loewe, pp. 75–92. This principle plays an important part in Maimonides' discussion of the end of the world and is discussed again in Chapter 6.

thing produces a change in another; it does not tell us how one thing brings about the existence of another. Existence, as Joseph Owens remarks, is taken for granted.[14]

According to Aristotle, first philosophy investigates being as being and the attributes that pertain to it by virtue of its nature. Of the various senses of being that are discussed at *Metaphysics* 5.7, the closest he comes to our understanding of existence is being as accident. In the statement "The man is musical," the predicate attaches to the subject by accident because there is nothing in the essence of man that implies the ability to play an instrument. After pointing out other ways in which something can be true accidentally, Aristotle concludes (*Metaphysics* 1017a18–21):[15] "Thus when one thing is said in an accidental sense to be another, this is either because both belong to the same thing, and this is, or because that to which the attribute belongs is, or because the subject which has as an attribute that of which it is itself predicated, itself is."

The problem is that no science deals with things that happen by accident; rather, science deals with things that happen always or for the most part.[16] In fact, Aristotle goes so far as to suggest that the accidental is a mere name and in that sense akin to nonbeing.[17] It follows that if the existence of a thing is separate from its essence, so that knowledge of the latter implies nothing about the former, the study of being as accident is outside the scope of philosophy. Thus, Owens is right to say that Aristotle would have had no interest in a free creation even if he believed it as a religious dogma.[18]

---

[14] Owens, *Doctrine*, p. 359.

[15] I am following the translation of W. D. Ross, *The Works of Aristotle Translated into English: Metaphysics.*

[16] Aristotle, *Metaphysics* 1026b4–5, 1027a20–22. For more on this point, see Charles H. Kahn, "The Greek Verb 'To Be' and the Concept of Being," *Foundations of Language* 2 (1966), especially p. 250: "For the philosophical usage of the verb, the most fundamental value of *einai* when used alone (without predicates) is not 'to exist' but 'to be so,' 'to be the case,' or to be true."

[17] Aristotle, *Metaphysics* 1026b13–21.

[18] Owens, *The Doctrine of Being*, p. 467.

That is not to deny that Aristotle had the resources to distinguish *what* a thing is from *that* a thing is, because he clearly does.[19] But he makes this distinction in a methodological context dealing with the distinction between a definition and a demonstration; he does not use it as a basis for saying that existence is primary. That is why he never asks the question "Why is there something rather than nothing?" and asks instead, "Why is there eternal motion?" For him the goal of philosophy is not to investigate the origin of the world but its structure.

Needless to say, some in antiquity saw things differently. According to Simplicius, Proclus' criticism misses the mark. Like the Demiurge in Plato's *Timaeus*, Aristotle's God is responsible for the existence of the heavens as well as their motion.[20] Although this claim strikes us as dubious, it is important to recognize the context in which it was made. Long before Proclus or Simplicius came on the scene, philosophers opposed to skepticism recognized that part of the skeptics' strategy was to find discrepancies between the two leading authorities, Plato and Aristotle.[21] To respond to this argument, and thus to save philosophy as they understood it, opponents of skepticism set out to show that despite the different ways in which they expressed themselves, Plato and Aristotle could be combined to form a unified system of thought. In brief, one began with the *Organon*, *De Anima*, *Physics*, and *Metaphysics* and concluded with the middle books of the *Republic*, the *Timaeus*, and finally the *Parmenides*.

The doctrine of emanation was a prominent part of this system and allowed its adherents to explain how all of existence derives from a single source. Once this doctrine is in place, what seemed

---

[19] See for example *Posterior Analytics* 89b33 and 91a1. For further discussion, see Owens, *The Doctrine*, pp. 290–92.

[20] Simplicius, *On Aristotle's Physics* 1360, 24–1363, 24.

[21] The chief figure here is Antiochus of Ascalon (130 B.C.). For accounts of his life, see Eduard Zeller, *A History of Eclecticism in Greek Philosophy*, pp. 85–102; and John Dillon, *The Middle Platonists*, pp. 52–105.

to many as the missing link in Aristotle's philosophy was filled in: not only could he explain desire *for* God but the procession of the world *from* God. In this way, the Prime Mover became a kind of creator – not that he is responsible for a temporal creation but that he is responsible for the fact that there is a world at all.

The tendency to harmonize Plato and Aristotle was abetted by the dissemination of a number of pseudographic works attributed to Aristotle but containing selections from Neoplatonic sources. *Dicta of the Greek Sage, Letter Concerning Divine Science*, and *Theology of Aristotle* are basically summaries of *Enneads* 4–6, and *Liber de Causis* is a summary of Proclus' *Elements of Theology*.[22] The doctrines contained in these works seek to explain how the world as we know it emerged from a single source of infinite power and perfection.

Although Maimonides does not mention these works, he attributes to Aristotle and his followers the view that everything was brought into existence by God according to a necessary and eternal emanation. He even goes so far as to say that emanation provides a possible way to interpret the opening lines of Genesis (*GP* 2.25, pp. 327–28). In this view, what the Bible depicts as temporal creation is just a colorful way of describing the dependence of the world *on* God or its eternal procession *from* God. As the author of the *Theology* makes clear, the nature of the cause determines the nature of the effect: if the cause is eternal, the effect will be; if the cause is temporal, the effect will be as well.[23] Because God is eternal, both the manner in which the world comes to be and the world itself must also be eternal. It is clear, however, that despite Maimonides' respect for the Aristotelian tradition, he cannot accept the doctrine of emanation as it stands. If the effect must resemble

[22] For Greek texts and English translations of *The Greek Sage, Letter Concerning Divine Science*, and *Theology of Aristotle* (short form), see *Plotini Opera*, Vol. 2, ed. Paul Henry and Hans-Rudolph Schwyzer. For the *Liber de Causis*, see *The Book of Causes*, trans. Dennis J. Brand.

[23] *Theology of Aristotle* 45 (Henry and Schwyzer, p. 231).

the cause, how can a simple, immaterial being be responsible for a complex, material world?

In keeping with this tradition, Maimonides admits at *GP* 1.69 that God is the efficient, formal, and final cause of the world by virtue of giving it existence. Thus: "The universe exists in virtue of the existence of the Creator, and the latter continually endows it with permanence in virtue of the thing that is spoken of as overflowing... Accordingly if the nonexistence of the Creator were supposed, all that exists would likewise be nonexistent" (p. 169). The chapter makes clear, however, that this discussion is provisional and that his main purpose is to raise the question of divine causality and distance himself from the Mutakallimūn.[24] Even here he continues to deny that there is an analogy between God and humans. If God is a form, or as Maimonides says, the ultimate form, God is still different from any of the forms that inhabit matter.

If, as I have suggested, Maimonides does not accept the doctrine of emanation, with what does he replace it? It is easy to say that he replaces it with a doctrine of temporal creation, but the logic of this position is far from clear, and many people are of the opinion that he defends it only to satisfy traditional followers of the religion.[25]

I

In view of the problems discussed in the previous section, it might be tempting to say that we should leave philosophy and turn to prophecy. As Maimonides points out, philosophers have been

[24] For a different view of this chapter, see Warren Zev Harvey, "Why Maimonides Was Not a Mutakallim," *PM*, pp. 105–14, especially 113–14. In response to Harvey: (1) by Maimonides' own admission, *Guide* 1.69 is provisional, and (2) the question "Was Maimonides defending religion or seeking truth?" is too general and begs the question.

[25] See, for example, Shlomo Pines, "Translator's Introduction," *Guide of the Perplexed*, pp. cxxv–cxxxi; Warren Zev Harvey, "A Third Approach to Maimonides' Cosmology-Prophetology Puzzle," *M*, pp. 71–88.

discussing creation for three thousand years and still have not reached a definitive conclusion. Faced with a similar predicament, Aquinas argues that the doctrine of creation should be accepted on faith.[26] At *GP* 2.16 (p. 294), Maimonides says something similar: because the issue of creation remains open, the best strategy is to accept it on the authority of the prophets. Unfortunately things are not that simple. Although it is fair to say that the prophetic tradition upholds some view of creation, it is open to question what that view is.

In some places, the Bible reflects an older mythological tradition according to which God tamed unruly forces in what appears to have been a cosmic civil war. At Psalms 74:12–15 and Isaiah 51:9–10, for example, God is praised for slaying monsters and drying up the seas.[27] The opening lines of Genesis present a different picture: God fashions the world out of a watery chaos that is unformed and void (*tohu va-vohu*). Although natural forces such as water, wind, darkness, and the face of the deep (*tehom*) are mentioned, none put up any opposition to God. All God has to do is say something, and immediately it is so.

Even if we grant that God's sovereignty is unchallenged, problems remain. First there is the question of order. Although Genesis 1:1 says that God created the heavens and the earth, Genesis 2.4 says that God made the earth and the heavens. Is the order significant? Philo argued that the heavens were created first because they are the best and purest thing in all of creation.[28] Various rabbis took opposites sides. The school of Shammai argued that the heavens came first, the school of Hillel that the earth did, and Rabbi Simeon ben Yohai said they were created simultaneously, indicating that they are of equal importance.[29]

---

[26] *ST* 1.46.2.

[27] Also see Psalms 89:9–13; Job 26:7, 38:4–39:30.

[28] Philo, *On Creation* 27–28.

[29] *Genesis Rabbah* 1.15.

Then there is the question of raw materials. Although God created the heavens and the earth, we are not told how or from what. A rabbinic dispute ensued on whether they were made independently of each other or whether one was made out of the other.[30] One tradition holds that heaven and earth were made from *tohu* and *vohu*.[31] According to Rav, *tohu* and *vohu* were created first, from them came darkness and water, then light and fire, then heaven.[32] The earth emerged when the waters of the sea withdrew. Another tradition (narrated from one rabbi to another in a whisper) maintains that God stretched out the heavens like a tent and clothed himself in light as in a garment.[33] Along similar lines, Rabbi Eliezer claims that the heavens were made from the light of God's garment, and the earth was made from the snow under the throne of glory.[34]

Obviously passages that mention materials such as wind or water are ambiguous, because even if we suppose that God made the world out of them, there is still the question of whether they themselves are created or eternal.[35] Commenting on the theory of Rabbi Eliezer, Maimonides (*GP* 2.26, p. 331) says that we should ask him from what the light of the garment, the snow, and the throne of glory were created. Some rabbis went so far as to say that multiple worlds were created before this one, implying that materials from one were used to fashion another.[36] Not everyone looked at the matter this way, however. In response to an unnamed

---

[30] *Genesis Rabbah* 12.2.

[31] *Genesis Rabbah* 1.5.

[32] Ibid.

[33] *Genesis Rabbah* 4.5; for the biblical reference, see Psalms 104:1–3.

[34] *Chapters of Rabbi Eliezer* 3.

[35] There is a debate on whether Philo believed that the preexistent matter out of which the world was created was itself created. Wolfson (*Philo*, Vol. 1, pp. 300–12) argues that it was, but David Winston (*Philo of Alexandria*, pp. 7–21) argues otherwise. For more on the history of creation *ex nihilo*, see Wolfson, *The Philosophy of the Kalam*, pp. 355–72.

[36] *Genesis Rabbah* 3.7, 9.2.

philosopher who said that God needed the assistance of *tohu, vohu,* darkness, water, wind, and the deep to create the world, Rabbi Gamaliel maintained that everything was created, a statement that some have taken as an early expression of creation *ex nihilo.*[37]

Even a simple reading of Genesis 1:1–2 shows that either view is possible. If we interpret the text as "In the beginning God created the heavens and the earth. [And then] the earth was unformed and void," God is the sole agent, and the shaping of matter takes place after the initial act of creation. If we take it as "When God created the heavens and the earth, the earth was unformed and void," creation *is* the shaping of matter. As is well known, the grammar of the passage has been disputed for centuries. The first word (*bereshit*) is a noun in the construct state. Instead of being followed by a second noun in the absolute state, which is the normal pattern, it is followed by a verb. For this reason, Rashi takes the passage to mean, "In the beginning of God's creation of the heavens and the earth, when the earth was unformed and void...."[38] On this reading, the heavens and the earth are not the first things to exist, because the passage says that the spirit of God hovered over the face of the waters during creation. Following a well-established rabbinic doctrine, Rashi maintains that the heavens (*shamayim*) were made from water (*mayim*) and fire (*esh*).[39] Although it is not clear how fire enters the picture, this interpretation implies that water and fire were present when creation began.

[37] *Genesis Rabbah* 1.9. See Alexander Altmann, "A Note on the Rabbinic Doctrine of Creation," *Studies in Religious Philosophy and Mysticism,* p. 129. Altmann's interpretation is challenged by David Winston, "The Book of Wisdom's Theory of Cosmogony," *History of Religions* 11 (1971–72): 188–191. According to Winston, Rabbi Gamaliel was not objecting to preexistent matter but to the Gnostic idea that there were multiple powers at work in creation. In response to Winston: (1) The text is too abbreviated to know exactly what Rabbi Gamaliel's opponent believes, and (2) it is not clear that the distinction between preexistent matter and creative powers other than God is significant, because in either case God becomes a joint cause of the world's existence rather than a sole cause.

[38] For a similar reading, see Gersonides, *WL* 6.2.8, p. 449.

[39] See *Genesis Rabbah* 4.7.

The biblical scholar Richard Friedman argues that the passage should not read "the earth was unformed and void" but "the earth had been unformed and void."[40] This means that the earth was in a shapeless, formless condition prior to creation and thus preceded creation. Like Rashi, Friedman concludes that the Torah is not trying to take us back to a radical beginning of time but to describe the origin of an orderly world out of chaos. The closest we get to creation *ex nihilo* in the text of Genesis is 1:3: "God said, 'Let there be light.' And there was light." Yet this, too, raises questions. Because heavenly bodies do not appear until the fourth day, it is unclear what this light is, from what it derives, or whether it was preceded by darkness. In Friedman's view, the daylight that surrounds the earth does not derive from the sun but is an independent creation of God for which no material source is given. We saw, however, that one rabbinic tradition holds that light was created from the garment in which God wrapped himself. According to Alexander Altmann, in this tradition *garment* is a metaphor for *aspect* or *attribute*. If so, what these rabbis are saying is that light is an emanation or effulgence that proceeds from divine wisdom.[41]

In regard to cosmology, the opening verses present a picture according to which the earth is a large bubble surrounded by water. Inside the bubble is dry land that is surrounded by seas. Above the land and seas is the sky, which inhabits a domelike structure or firmament. Above and around the firmament is more water. Although the text does not mention the use of instruments in creation, rabbinic commentaries, following Proverbs 3:19 and 8:22–31, argue that the Torah antedated creation and served as a blueprint.[42]

Last but not least is the question of what creation means. From what we have seen, divine activity involves both the shaping of formless matter and the calling of things into existence. From an

[40] Richard Eliott Friedman, *Commentary on the Torah*, p. 5.
[41] Altmann, *Studies*, pp. 132–39.
[42] *Pirke Avot* 3:18.

etymological standpoint, the word *bara* (create) is used only of God, so it is difficult to say with precision what is intended. To complicate matters, Genesis also says that God *made* the firmament (1:7) and all of creation (1:31), *separated* light from darkness (1:4), and *formed* man from the dust of the earth (2:7). Isaiah (48:13) says that God spread out the heavens and formed light (45:7). Does this indicate that God engaged in several kinds of activities during the first six days, or are these words different names for the same thing? More important for our purposes, is creation fundamentally different from the production of one existing thing from another? If so, the first sentence of Genesis stands apart from everything else. Once the world comes to be, we no longer have creation but activities akin to the actions of a craftsman.

According to Maimonides, *create* is connected to nonbeing and therefore refers to creation *ex nihilo*, whereas *make* refers to the giving of specific forms or natures, and form refers to the giving of accidents.[43] Because these distinctions presuppose metaphysical categories that are never explicitly mentioned in the Bible, it is doubtful that the original audience would have known what he was getting at. Along these lines, David Winston argues that there is no clear reference to creation *ex nihilo* until the second century A.D., and then it arises not as a Jewish interpretation of Scripture but as a Christian response to Gnosticism.[44]

---

[43] For Maimonides on *bara*, see *GP* 2.30, p. 358; 3.10, p. 438. For detailed analysis of Maimonides' use of *bara*, see Sara Klein-Braslavy, "Maimonides' Interpretation of the Verb *Bara* and the Problem of the Creation of the World" (in Hebrew), *Da'at* 16 (1986): 39–55, as well "The Creation of the World and Maimonides' Interpretation of Gen. I–V," *MP*, pp. 65–71. As Klein-Braslavy observes, Maimonides associates *bara* with creation out of nothing (*min 'adam*). The problem is that *'adam* is ambiguous: it can be used in an absolute sense, in which case it means nothing, or a relative one, in which it means matter or privation. I have more to say about this issue in Chapter 3.

[44] Winston, "The Book," p. 191. Against Winston, see Jonathan Goldstein ("The Origins of the Doctrine of Creation Ex Nihilo," *Journal of Jewish Studies* 35 (1984): 127–35), who thinks that the doctrine first arose as a consequence of belief in bodily resurrection.

As one might expect, the evidence is mixed. Some see a hint of creation *ex nihilo* in Isaiah 45:6–7: "I form light and create darkness."[45] In other words, God is the source of everything, not just form or structure. A few lines later (45:18–19) Isaiah suggests that, contrary to a literal reading of Genesis, there was no chaos at the beginning. Although some see a reference to creation *ex nihilo* at 2 Maccabees 7:28, where creation proceeds "not from existent things" (*ouk ex ontōn*), or in some texts "from nonexistent things" (*ex ouk ontōn*), the meaning is also unclear because the key phrase can be taken in an absolute sense, in which case it refers to nothing, or a relative one, in which case it refers to extreme privation of matter.[46] By contrast, the *Wisdom of Solomon* (11:17) says that the world was created out of formless matter (*ex amorphou hulēs*).

Even when the idea of creation *ex nihilo* came on the scene, a debate arose on what *ex nihilo* means. Those who had trouble imagining how something could be produced from nothing maintained that it meant the world was created out of the essence of God; others went the full distance and maintained that nothing should be understood as radical nothingness.[47] By the same token, some thought that God contains in himself all the forms, of everything that exists, so that creation proceeds by emanation; whereas others thought that God contains no forms, so that creation proceeds by divine fiat.[48] In view of this evidence, there is no reason to think that the Bible was trying to formulate a consistent doctrine of how the world came to be. Rather than delve into the mechanics

[45] Moshe Weinfeld, "God the Creator in Gen. 1 and in the Prophecy of Second Isaiah" (in Hebrew), *Tarbiz* 37 (1968): 120–32.

[46] On this point, see Wolfson, *Studies in the History and Philosophy of Religion*, Vol. 1, pp. 212–13; Klein-Braslavy, "The Creation," ibid.; Samuelson, *Judaism and the Doctrine of Creation*, pp. 101–2; and Seeskin, *SFDG*, pp. 71–72.

[47] For a discussion of the various alternatives, see Wolfson's treatment of Gregory of Nyssa, *SHPR*, Vol. 1, pp. 199–206, as well as the history of creation *ex nihilo* in pp. 207–21.

[48] On this distinction, see Ammonius' "On the Opinions of the Philosophers," in *Isaac Israeli*, trans. A. Altmann and S. M. Stern, pp. 70–71.

of creation, the opening lines of Genesis try to establish God as the undisputed master of the world. This is why they are so short on detail. The simple phrases that comprise the narrative – "God made," "God separated," and so forth – are noteworthy mainly for what they leave out: any reference to instruments, intermediaries, opposing forces, or magical incantations – in short, the stuff of mythology.

With such an abbreviated account at their disposal, the rabbis had ample opportunity to speculate on the how and why of creation. Although such speculation may have been informed by exposure to Hellenistic philosophy, for them the primary reason for talking about creation is homiletic: to stress the glory of God so that people will be motivated to live by the word of God. If one can derive a scientific message in the process, so be it; but that is not their primary intention. Urbach argues that although the rabbis broadened the scope of the creation discussion by filling in details, the influence of Neoplatonism, Gnosticism, and other creation "dramas" is still muted.[49] It is from these commentaries that we get the picture of God as "He who spoke and the world came into being," in short, the view that God created the world by fiat. The precedent for this can be found as early as Psalms 33:6–9: "By the word of the Lord the heavens were made. . . . He spoke, and it came to be."

Even something as simple as an epithet can have consequences. If heaven and earth, sun and moon, living creatures, and human beings are created, then whatever the nature of that creation, the things that result are products of divine activity, not divine themselves. Thus Rabbi Gamaliel's insight: if God needed the help of material forces to create the world, the glory of God would be diminished. Another rabbinic commentary claims that *et* (a word indicating the presence of a direct object) is needed in the first

---

[49] Ephraim Urbach, *The Sages*, pp. 212–13.

sentence so that we should not think that heaven and earth are divine powers existing alongside God.[50]

Simply put, God is not a partner of rain, wind, sky, or water, but their source. To suppose otherwise is to conceive of God along the lines of a Demiurge. In keeping with the thought of Isaiah 40, all things are as nothing before God. It is that conviction rather than unambiguous textual evidence that led people to say that although there is no explicit mention of creation *ex nihilo* in Genesis, when we take into account the unique status it assigns to God, creation *ex nihilo* is implied.[51] If creation is the shaping of eternal matter, it would resemble the human construction of artifacts, with the obvious consequence that the glory of God would be compromised. In short, the issue is theological rather than grammatical. Whatever conceptual problems there may be with creation *ex nihilo*, from a religious perspective, it has one overriding virtue: it directs attention away from the world and focuses it entirely on God. By the Middle Ages, even Abraham ibn Ezra, who did not believe in creation *ex nihilo*, acknowledged that most biblical commentators did.[52]

II

The conclusion just reached sits well with Maimonides' claim that creation is an integral part of monotheism. Where Maimonides parts company with a modern approach is that he thinks Genesis does contain a consistent doctrine that can be studied and

---

[50] *Hagigah* 12a; *Genesis Rabbah* 1.14.

[51] See, for example, Yehezkel Kauffman (*The Religion of Ancient Israel*, p. 68), who argues that the opening lines of Genesis represent a "clear poetic expression" of creation *ex nihilo*. Also see Nahum Sarna, *The JPS Torah Commentary: Genesis*, p. 5.

[52] See ibn Ezra's commentary on Genesis 1. For an English translation, see ibn Ezra's *Commentary on the Pentateuch: Genesis*, trans. H. Norman Strickman and Arthur M. Silver. Part of ibn Ezra's argument is that *bara* does not refer to creation *ex nihilo* at Genesis 1:1, because it is not used that way at Genesis 1:27 and Isaiah 45:7. But Genesis 1:27, which talks about the creation of humans, is ambiguous, whereas Isaiah 45:7 is hard to interpret, because it talks about the creation of darkness.

defended. In fact, he identifies *ma'aseh bereshit* (the account of the beginning) with the science of physics. As one might expect, he approaches the text of Genesis with a specific doctrine in mind. According to *GP* 2.30 (p. 349): "I have already made it known to you that the foundation of the whole Law is the view that God has brought the world into being out of nothing."

The bulk of Maimonides' interpretation of Genesis 1 occurs at *GP* 2.30, after the philosophic reasons for believing in creation have been examined. For purposes of exposition, I will reverse the textual order and look at his Bible commentary first. He begins by distinguishing two types of priority: causal and temporal. To avoid misunderstanding, it would be best to think of causality in the broad sense of providing a ground or principle (Greek: *archē*; Arabic: *mabda'*) rather than the narrow sense of an efficient cause. In this way, the heart is the cause or principle of a living being, and an element is the cause or principle of a compound. In both cases, the cause is prior to the effect because the effect could not exist without the cause. With respect to temporal priority, sometimes there is causal efficacy and sometimes not. A seed is both causally and temporally prior to a full-grown plant; by contrast, the first occupant of a house is temporally prior to a later one but does not function as a cause. As Maimonides indicates, the Hebrew word that signifies temporal priority is *tehillah,* whereas that signifying causal priority is *reshit,* which is derived from the word for head (*rosh*).

Maimonides clearly rejects the idea of a temporal beginning of the world if that means creation is a process that takes place in or over time. Throughout Book Two of the *Guide,* he assumes that time is an accident dependent on motion, so that if there is no motion, there can be no time either – thus, no time before the world was created.[53] He repeats this sentiment at *GP* 2.30 (p. 349): "Now

[53] *GP* 2.13, p. 281–2.

the world has not been created in a temporal beginning, as we have explained, for time belongs to the created things." If the Mosaic view of creation were committed to preexistent time, there *would* be no point in discussing it.[54] Because Maimonides obviously does discuss it, we have no choice but to say that it regards time as created.

Maimonides goes on to say that in *bereshit* (*be*+*reshit*) the prefix should be interpreted as "in" (*fī*) and claims that the first line of Genesis should read: "In the origin (*bad'a*) God created what is high and low." Unfortunately, this, too, is ambiguous. As Gersonides notes, the root *reshit* can express temporal priority, priority of order or importance, priority of rank, or causal priority.[55]

In view of Maimonides' repeated assertions that belief in creation is a foundation of the Law, I think we have to take him as saying that in Genesis 1:1 *bereshit* implies both temporal and causal priority. Hence the claim (ibid.) that his reading of the passage "fits in with creation in time [*ḥudūth*]." I have argued that Pines complicates matters by translating *ḥudūth* as "creation in time," something Maimonides says repeatedly that he rejects.[56] It would

---

[54] Here I am in agreement with Norbert Samuelson, "Maimonides' Doctrine of Creation," *Harvard Theological Review* 84 (1993), p. 253. I disagree, however, with the claim (p. 253) that there never was a time when there was no universe. We will see that according to Maimonides, purpose and particularization imply that something that did not exist is brought into existence.

[55] WL 6.2.2. For more on the history of the ambiguity, see Seymour Feldman, "An Averroist Solution to a Maimonidean Perplexity," *MS* 4 (2000): 18. As Feldman indicates, it is possible to read the passage as saying that *be* should be taken in an instrumental sense and translated as "with." This would mean that God created the world with an instrument. The problem, as Feldman recognizes, is that Maimonides never says what this instrument is. The Averroist reading of Albalag conflicts with Maimonides' stated preference for creation *de novo*. In Feldman's words (p. 15): "Maimonides explicitly and vigorously defends the doctrine of creation *ex nihilo* as the view of the Torah." The crux of Albalag's reading is that *ḥudūth* must be interpreted as continual recreation rather than creation *de novo*.

[56] SFDG, pp. 73–74. Harvey ("A Third Approach to Maimonides' Cosmogony-Prophetology Puzzle," *M*, p. 77) takes *GP* 2.30 to rule out a temporal creation. This is true if "temporal creation" refers to a process that occurs over time and takes place in time. It is not true if it means that both time and motion began with creation.

be better to say his reading of Genesis 1:1 fits in with creation *de novo*, which he characterizes at *Guide* 2.13 (p. 285) as the view that there is nothing eternal in any way existing simultaneously with God.[57] In any case, the dependence of time on motion does not imply that both are eternal. Although the world may exist throughout all time, it is still possible to say that time is finite, having been brought into existence at a particular point.

This point was made as early as Augustine:[58]

> The world was made not in time but together with time. For, what is made in time is made after one period and before another, namely, after a past and before a future time. But, there could have been no past time, since there was nothing created by whose movements and change time could be measured.

If time and motion are created together, creation marks the beginning of time rather than something that takes place in or through time. Maimonides' reason for saying he rejects temporal priority is that God does not precede the world in the way that one occupant of a house precedes another or a father precedes his son. God is not in time at all, so it is misleading to speak of a temporal relation between God and something else.[59]

But surely Maimonides expects us to see that God's priority goes beyond that which obtains between the heart and the body or an element and a compound. Although the heart may be a vital part of the body and the source of its life, no one would argue that it is the agent by which the body comes to be.[60] Yet this is exactly what Maimonides does say about God. The world is completely

---

[57] On the need to distinguish creation *de novo* from creation *ex nihilo*, see William Dunphy, "Maimonides and Aquinas on Creation: A Critique of Their Historians," in *Graceful Reason*, ed. Lloyd P. Gerson, pp. 361–79.

[58] Augustine, *City of God* 11.6.

[59] *GP* 1.57, p. 133. Cf. Plotinus, *EN* 3.7.2.

[60] Maimonides himself expresses reservations about this analogy at *GP* 1.72, pp. 192–93.

dependent on God: it can neither bring itself into existence nor keep itself there without God's help. In his words from *GP* 1.69 (p. 169): "He is that upon which the existence and stability of every form in the world ultimately reposes and by which they are constituted." In short, Maimonides needs a stronger form of causal priority than what his examples provide. This becomes clear when he claims that the priority he is talking about is compatible with creation *de novo*. I suggest, therefore, that according to Maimonides, *bereshit* has to imply temporal as well as causal priority. God is not just the principle that underlies the world but the agent that brought the world into existence. Whether it also implies creation *ex nihilo* remains to be seen.

As I indicated earlier, there was a rabbinic tradition that argued for the creation of worlds before this one. Maimonides connects this tradition with Aristotle, who argues that the idea of a first instant in time is incoherent, so that as far back as one can go, there is always a prior moment.[61] In Maimonides' opinion, the reason for this is that they took literally the references to "one day," "a second day," and so on. Then they reasoned that if there was as yet no sun or rotating sphere, there could not be a day. They concluded that there must have been temporal order before the creation of this world, which implies that there must have been a prior world. Not surprisingly, Maimonides rejects this claim because it is paradoxical and because, in his opinion, it contradicts the foundation of the Law. Note that even if there were a world before this one, the question of its origin would arise, and we would be asking all over again whether the world is eternal or created *de novo*.

Maimonides discusses another rabbinic interpretation of Genesis, which takes the opening sentence as: "In the beginning, God created, together with the heavens, everything that is in the heavens, and together with the earth, everything that is in the earth."

---

[61] I have more to say on this argument in the next chapter.

This coincides with his description of the Mosaic view of creation at *GP* 2.13 (p. 281), which holds that God brought forth "all the beings as they are." If so, the debates over what came first in creation are beside the point because everything was created at once, and gradually things became differentiated. As he points out, it is like a farmer sowing different kinds of seeds: some will spring up right away, and others will take more time. The idea that God created everything together in the first instant of time contrasts with the view that a long chain of causal connections followed from the necessity of the divine nature. As we will see, Maimonides rejects the latter as an account of the origin of the world and expresses sympathy with the rabbinic view.

Two consequences follow. First, for Maimonides the designations "one day," "a second day," and so on cannot be taken literally.[62] The real act of creation is described in the first sentence, when God brings everything into existence. After that, all we have is the actualization of potential. We can think of the actualization of potential in narrative form if we like, but the fact remains that creation itself is an instantaneous act. Once this point is made, the motivation for positing a temporal order prior to creation vanishes. Second, the creation of the world is fundamentally different from changes that occur within it. One has to do with the giving of existence, the other with growth and development. We will see in a later chapter that this distinction is critical for Maimonides' case against Aristotle because it implies that the causes and principles that explain growth and development cannot explain creation. Like God, creation is unique.

If references to days cannot be taken literally, neither can references to elements. According to Maimonides, *earth* is an equivocal term referring to all elements beneath the sphere of the moon

---

[62] Here I am in general agreement with the conclusions of Sara Klein-Braslavy, *Maimonides' Interpretation*, pp. 251–55.

and to the lowest element in particular. When Genesis says that the earth was unformed and void, it uses the term in the general sense; when it says that God called the dry land *earth*, it uses it in the specific. The opening lines mention earth, water, spirit or air (*ruah*), and darkness, which Maimonides takes as a listing of the traditional elements according to their natural position: earth, water, air, and fire. Fire is identified with darkness on the basis of textual considerations and because the elemental fire is not luminous; if it were, we would see the sky ablaze all the time.[63] Thus, air is mentioned as being "over the face of the waters," and darkness is said to be "over the face of the deep," which Maimonides takes as meaning above the air. The darkness that refers to the elemental fire is then distinguished from the darkness that corresponds to night (Genesis 1:5).

Maimonides pursues a similar strategy in regard to water. The water over which God's spirit hovers at Genesis 1:2 is not the water that now composes the seas but the stuff from which God makes the water under the firmament, the firmament itself, and the water above the firmament. According to Genesis 1:7, God divided the waters that are under the firmament from the waters above it. Maimonides claims this is not just a case of separating things geographically but a case of creating two things with different natures. The water that is below the firmament and gathered together to form the seas (Genesis 1:10) is an earthly element. In his words (*GP* 2.30, pp. 352–53):[64]

> Thus it has become clear that there was a certain common matter, which it names water. Afterwards it was divided into three forms;

---

[63] The argument is based in part on the similarity between Deuteronomy 4:36 ("On earth he showed you his great fire, while you heard his words coming out of the fire") and Deuteronomy 5:20 ("While you heard the voice out of the darkness...").

[64] Maimonides was hardly alone in discussing the complexities of the Bible's treatment of water. See, for example, Aquinas, *ST* 1.68.2. For the history of the problem in Christian philosophy, see Edward Grant, *PSO*, 1200–1687, pp. 103–4, 332–34. For discussion of this issue in Jewish circles, see Klein-Braslavy, *Maimonides' Interpretation*, pp. 160–74.

a part of it turned into one thing, namely the seas; another part of it turned into another thing, namely the firmament; a third part turned into a thing that is above the firmament. The latter is entirely beyond the earth.

Although the water above the firmament is also called *water*, it has nothing but its name in common with the water we drink or sail on. Maimonides points out that this conclusion is reinforced by the fact that it is physically impossible for earthly water to be suspended above the air.

What, then, is the water above the firmament? The most reasonable suggestion is that it is earthly water *in potentia* and becomes actualized when rain falls. According to Genesis 7:11, the great flood came when the fountains of the deep burst forth and the windows in the heavens opened. Is the water above the firmament fluid? If so, we again face the question of what holds it up. Is it solid or crystalline? If so, it must be luminous and transparent like ice. Maimonides is not explicit on this subject, except to say that the biblical text cannot be taken literally so that *water* must be regarded as an equivocal term. As for the firmament, some see it as part of the atmosphere, while others see it as the outermost sphere.[65]

Despite these ambiguities, the general direction of Maimonides' interpretation is clear: he wants to show that after we get past the first sentence, the opening verses of Genesis are based on the principles of Aristotelian physics. As he makes clear at *GP* 2.29 (p. 346), not everything mentioned in the opening verses of Genesis should be taken in its simple or external sense "as the vulgar imagine," for if that were the case, there would be no reason that one is prevented from discussing it in their presence. To a modern reader, a connection between Aristotle and Genesis seems wild and insupportable. We should keep in mind, however, that Maimonides is operating

---

[65] For the former interpretation, see Klein-Braslavy, ibid.; for the latter, see Y. Tzvi Langermann, "Maimonides and Astronomy: Some Further Reflections," in Langermann, *The Jews and the Sciences in the Middle Ages*, p. 11.

with a different hermeneutics. For him the Torah is not a man-made document reflecting the attitudes of the people who wrote it but a source of eternal truth. He is perfectly willing to change his interpretation of the Torah if it can be demonstrated that what he had previously ascribed to it is false.[66]

Although Maimonides has doubts about Aristotle's celestial physics, he has few doubts about Aristotle's earthly physics. In the words of GP 2.24, p. 326: "All that Aristotle states about that which is beneath the sphere of the moon is in accordance with reasoning (qiyās)." This is why he thinks he has done his reader a service by showing that Genesis is compatible with it. Without Maimonides' interpretation, the reader would be stuck with an obscure text made even more obscure by the plethora of conflicting interpretations that have grown up around it. Underlying Maimonides' hermeneutics is his conviction that the external sense of a passage is not always the true one and that we should not assume that key words always refer to the same thing, a conviction that has ample support in rabbinic literature.

### III

There are two reasons creation is important. The religious reason is that once we accept a necessary being who is responsible for the existence of everything else, the question of origin becomes central. It will no longer do to take the existence of the world for granted. The philosophic reason has to do with priority: before we can answer questions about the structure of the world, we have to tackle the question of why there is a world at all.[67] To do this, we have to consider the possibility that the world might not exist.

---

[66] GP 2.25, pp. 327–28.

[67] It is true that Maimonides avails himself of a version of the cosmological argument that assumes eternal motion. But (1) this proof is supplemented by others in which the existence or nonexistence of the world is critical, for example GP, 2.1, pp. 247–48; (2) unlike Aristotle's, Maimonides' proof from eternal motion is not his last word

With the benefit of hindsight, we can say that the opening lines of Genesis provide the impetus for both insights. For the first time, we are presented with a God who rules all of existence and brings things into being by issuing commands. According to Gilson, we are also presented with an early version of the distinction between essence and existence.[68] In an eternal world like that described in Greek philosophy, Gilson maintains, an essence is eternally realized and inconceivable except as realized. In a created world like that described in Genesis, this is not so. Essences are neutral with respect to existence in the sense that they remain the same whether or not they are instantiated. This is another way of saying that no finite essence can supply a reason why something embodies it.

Following Avicenna, Maimonides concludes that if existence is separate from essence, it should be understood as an accident (*'araḍ*) that attaches to what exists.[69] As Altmann points out, this does not mean that existence attaches to the essence of things, because that would commit Maimonides to a form of Platonism in which essences such as man, horse, or dog exist on their own.[70] Rather, existence is an accident of the concrete individual, that in

on the subject but part of a dialectical strategy that argues as follows: If the world is eternal, God exists. If the world is created, God exists. Therefore, God exists.

[68] Etienne Gilson, *The Spirit of Medieval Philosophy*, p. 436. It could be argued that Platonic forms are separate from and exist independently of the things that partake in them. Still, Plato does not concern himself with unrealized essences in the sense that a medieval philosopher would use that term. There is, for example, no discussion of a form for imaginary creatures, possible worlds, or anything of the sort. Cf. Charles H. Kahn, "Why Existence Does Not Emerge as a Distinct Concept in Greek Philosophy," *Philosophies of Existence: Ancient and Medieval*, ed. Parviz Morewedge, p. 7: "My general view of the historical development is that existence in the modern sense becomes a central concept in philosophy only in the period when Greek ontology is radically revised in the light of a metaphysics of creation: that is to say under the influence of Biblical religion."

[69] See *GP* 1.57, p. 132; cf. 1.46, p. 97. For Avicenna's distinction, see *Al-Shifā'* 1.5, pp. 31–32. Strictly speaking, existence is not an accident of essence, because that would commit Maimonides to Platonism, a theory he rejects at *GP* 3.18. Rather existence is an accident of the concrete individual, that is, that in which the essence is embodied.

[70] Altmann, "Essence and Existence in Maimonides," *M*, pp. 148–65. Although Averroes criticized this doctrine, Altmann (p. 163, n. 3) argues that there is no solid evidence

which essences such as man, horse, or dog are embodied. Because the reason for the existence of a finite thing must be sought in something other than the essence, eventually all talk of existence must culminate in a God who exists necessarily and confers existence on other things.

Because no finite thing has an inherent right to exist, Maimonides claims the fact that it does is evidence of divine graciousness (ḥesed).[71] Elsewhere he connects the doctrine of creation with Psalms 145:9: "The Lord is good to all; and His tender mercies are over all His works." Obviously he was not the first person to make this move. Avicenna also claims that the essences of finite things have no inherent right to be.[72] We will see, however, that while Avicenna ascribes will to God, Maimonides does not think he is justified in doing so. For Maimonides the ascription of will makes sense only if God is free to create or not. Simply put, Maimonides regards existence as a gift. Once we grant that it is, the practice of offering thanks to God is not a hollow ritual but a legitimate response to a metaphysical truth. This does not mean that we can influence God through prayer but that we recognize that but for God, we are nothing.

The conceptual machinery needed to ask, "Why is there something rather than nothing?" took centuries to develop. Despite Gilson's contention that the germ of the insight is already present in Genesis, we saw that the text is hardly a model of clarity. To get to the point where it makes sense to speak of an unbroken line of development from a single sentence to a new worldview, one has to fill in a large number of gaps. From Gilson's perspective, Maimonides is one of them.

that Maimonides knew of Averroes' arguments when he wrote the *Guide* or that he accepted them later on.

[71] *GP* 3.53, p. 631.
[72] Avicenna, *Al-Shifā'* 8.6, p. 356.

# God and the Problem of Origin

We also saw that Maimonides seems to paint himself into a corner in regard to divine causality. The point of discussing the origin of the world is to argue that it has its origin in God. But once we see that God is not a substance possessing multiple attributes, the normal way of explaining causal interaction between God and the world falls apart. Unless Maimonides can find a way to explain it, he would be faced with two choices: (1) give up the question of origin and return to the question of structure or (2) retain the question of origin and soften the consequences of negative theology at least to the point of finding something that God has in common with the world. I take it that neither would be acceptable. It could be said, therefore, that Maimonides' entire philosophy hangs in the balance.

We can compare Maimonides' view of creation with his view of proving the existence of God. Like Aquinas, he believes that we can know that God exists but not what God is. Thus, knowledge of God is inferential: we begin with what we can see and infer the existence of something that lies beyond it. If my interpretation is right, much the same is true of creation: we have grounds for believing that it occurred even though we cannot say how. Still, these grounds are not as firm as one might like. Maimonides' strategy is to show that while doubts can be raised about either creation or eternity, more doubts can be raised about eternity. According to *GP* 2.17 (p. 294): "I shall make it clear that just as a certain disgrace attaches to us because of the belief in the creation in time, an even greater disgrace attaches to the belief in eternity." In Maimonides' hands, then, the question of origin is not factual ("How did the world come to be?") but conceptual ("Is it possible for the world to come to be?"). Is it reasonable to think that a simple, immaterial being possessing free will is responsible for the complex material world we inhabit?

The crux of his argument is that creation is different from generation and corruption. Generation and corruption are natural

33

processes adequately explained in terms of matter, form, and privation, or, more generally, act and potency. His argument is that serious doubts can be raised about whether such processes have any bearing on the question of creation. Why should we believe that the origin of the world resembles the origin of a natural thing within it? Before we go into the details of his argument, we must look at the philosophic sources from which he drew.

# 2

# Creation in the *Timaeus*

ALTHOUGH ARABIC TRANSLATIONS OF PLATO'S *TIMAEUS* were circulating in some form or other by the ninth century, it is unclear how much of the dialogue Maimonides knew.[1] The best guess is that he did not have a full text or line-by-line commentary and may have relied on paraphrases or secondary sources.[2] He lists

---

[1] For the Islamic world's knowledge of Plato, see al-Nadīm, *The Fihrist, A Tenth Century Survey of Muslim Culture*, trans. B. Dodge, p. 593, as well as F. Rosenthal, "On the Knowledge of Plato's Philosophy in the Islamic World," *Islamic Culture* 14 (1940): 384–422. For Maimonides' familiarity with portions of Galen's commentary on the *Timaeus* dealing with medical issues, see *Galeni in Platonis Timaeum Commentarii Fragmenta*, ed. H. O. Schröder, especially pp. 89–99.

[2] On this point, see Rosenthal, "On the Knowledge," p. 393: "Complete translations of Platonic Dialogues, therefore, according to the information obtainable from Arabic Bibliographies, were made very rarely. Not a single one of them has come down to us, and the character of those quotations which we have before us, never seems, as

Platonism as one of the three options for explaining the origin of the world but never cites the *Timaeus* directly, and in a letter written to Samuel ibn Tibbon complains that there are so many parables in Plato's writing one can dispense with it and stick to Aristotle.[3]

In view of this remark, we should not be surprised that at *GP* 2.13 and 2.15, Maimonides cites Aristotle's authority (presumably *Physics* 251b16–18) to argue that Plato believed the world was created and that the heavens are subject to generation and destruction.[4] What Aristotle actually says in that passage is that Plato alone believed that time was created and had a beginning together with the world. There is no mention of the destruction of the heavens. Moreover, at *De Caelo* 280a31–32, Aristotle criticizes Plato for holding that the heavens, although generated, will last forever.[5]

In the *Timaeus* itself (38b), Plato raises the possibility that the heavens will be destroyed but does so only to emphasize that time and the rotation of the heavens go hand in hand so that if you take away one, you take away both. Nothing indicates that having been created, they must eventually pass away.

> Time came into being together with the Heaven, in order that, as they were brought into being together, so they may be dissolved together, *if ever their dissolution should come to pass.* [my emphasis]

According to the narrator (37d), it is impossible for a created thing to be eternal, as the forms are, so the Demiurge sought to make a moving image of eternity and constructed an everlasting likeness

---

far as we can now judge, to afford grounds for the slightest probability that we are concerned with the remains of a pure and complete text of a Platonic Dialogue; therefore, a certain doubt may be entertained as to whether the translations mentioned were verbal reproductions of an unaltered Platonic wording."

[3] Two Hebrew versions of this letter can be found in A. Marx, "Texts by and about Maimonides," *Jewish Quarterly Review* N.S. 25 (1934): 378–80. Also see Shlomo Pines, "Translator's Introduction," *The Guide of the Perplexed*, lix.

[4] In the *Timaeus, heaven* or *the heaven* is often used as a synonym for the whole world and not a part of the world to be contrasted with earth. See, for example, 28b.

[5] The same sentiment is expressed at *Metaphysics* 1071b31–33.

that moves according to number; in short, he constructed time. Although Plato uses the world *aiōnios* to describe both the original and the copy, Cornford is right to suggest that we should understand the former as "eternal" and the latter as "everlasting."[6] In other words, the original is outside of time, whereas the copy is in time but indestructible. So there is little doubt that Plato's position is the one stated a bit later at *Timaeus* 38c: time and the heavens have been, are now, and will be for all time.

In fact later, at 41a–b, the Demiurge addresses the created gods by saying that while he could destroy them, only an evil will would want to do so and therefore "you shall not be dissolved nor taste death." The idea is that since these gods are created, they are not immortal or indestructible by nature. Nevertheless the Demiurge pledges to keep them in existence as an act of will.

In all likelihood Maimonides' view of Plato is based on his and Aristotle's conviction that whatever is generated according to nature must eventually pass away.[7] So certain is Maimonides of this point that at *GP* 2.27 (p. 332), he wonders how anyone could believe otherwise. As we will see, the answer is that the concept of generation is ambiguous. It can refer to temporal production, in which case Maimonides' and Aristotle's criticism has merit because experience confirms that things that are generated according to nature are also destroyed. But there was a long tradition of Neoplatonists who took generation to mean eternal dependence on something else. If that is what Plato meant, there is nothing implausible in the view that the heavens, although not self-sustaining, will last forever. As to the will of the Demiurge, it is hard to know whether this refers to a decision on the part of a cosmic agent

---

[6] F. M. Cornford, *Plato's Cosmology*, p. 98.

[7] See Aristotle, *De Caelo* 279b21: "Generated things are always seen to be destroyed." Cf. *GP* 2.14, p. 286; and *MT* 1, Basic Principles of the Torah, 4.3. The qualification *according to nature* is important because Maimonides believes that creation is not a natural process. Even though the world is created, it is eternal *a parte post*. I have more to say about this in Chapter 6.

or is intended as a metaphor for the fact that the heavens go on forever.

Like his view of Aristotle, Maimonides' view of Plato is more thematic than historical. In general, he associates Platonism with three claims: (1) creation *ex nihilo* is impossible, (2) the world had a beginning and was created from preexistent matter, and (3) the heavens are subject to generation and destruction. The most important of these claims is (2) because it allows Maimonides to say (*GP* 2.25, pp. 328–29) that unlike the Aristotelian view of creation, the Platonic one preserves belief in miracles and upholds the foundation of the Law. Although Maimonides does not have a great deal to say about the Platonic view, it is undeniable that the *Timaeus* played a major role in shaping the intellectual climate in which he lived.

It is clear, for example, that many of the rabbinic commentaries on Genesis are also committed to creation from preexistent matter, a fact that Maimonides observes in his discussion of Rabbi Eliezer.[8] Beyond this, the claim that the Demiurge looked to an eternal model in creating the world (28a–29a) may have inspired the rabbinic view that God looked to the Torah.[9] Finally, there is the idea that creation is a process of bringing order and purpose out of disorder. A biblical commentator who read the *Timaeus'* account of disorderly motion might well conclude that it is an apt description of *tohu va-vohu* in Genesis 1. "Many obscure passages," Maimonides (*GP* 2.25, p. 329) writes, "can be found in the texts of the Torah and others with which this opinion [Plato's] could be connected or rather by means of which it could be proved." Still, Maimonides insists that those who think he believes the same thing as Plato are mistaken, for he believes in creation *ex nihilo* whereas Plato does not.[10]

---

[8] See, however, J. C. M. van Winden, *Calcidius on Matter*, pp. 52–53, where Calcidius reports that the Jews believe that matter is generated.

[9] Maimonides draws a comparison between Plato and various rabbinic texts at *GP* 2.6, p. 263.

[10] *GP* 2.12, pp. 283–84. Some people think that despite this claim, Maimonides accepted, or may have accepted, the Platonic position. See Herbert Davidson,

I

As with Maimonides' view of Genesis, the *Timaeus* is shrouded in metaphor. The Demiurge, "maker and father of all things" (28c), is described as an artisan who deliberates about what he is going to do; makes artistic decisions, bends, shapes, or arranges raw materials; and takes pleasure in his work. According to 30a:[11]

> Desiring, then, that all things should be good and, so far as might be, nothing imperfect, the god took over all that is visible – not at rest, but in discordant and unordered motion – and brought it from disorder into order, since he judged that order was in every way better.

This suggests that the Demiurge deliberated about the creation of the world and exercised some degree of choice. If so, Maimonides' claim that the Platonic view of creation upholds the foundation of the Law has merit. The ensuing account of the origin of soul has the Demiurge mix portions of Sameness, Difference, and Being as if they were the ingredients in a loaf of bread. The cosmic forces, Reason (*nous*) and Necessity (*ananke*), are brought together like two mythological deities at 48a, at which point Reason overrules Necessity by persuading it to help guide sensible things to a good end. The receptacle is compared to a piece of gold, the base of a perfume, a mother, a nurse, and finally a foster mother. The chaotic motion of the receptacle before the Demiurge imposes order is compared to a winnowing basket in which vestiges (*ichne*) of earth, air, fire, and water are shaken, causing heavy pieces to go one way and light ones the other.

"Maimonides' Secret Position on Creation," in *Studies in Medieval Jewish History and Literature*, ed. I. Twersky, pp. 16–40; Alfred Ivry, "Maimonides on Creation," in *Creation and the End of Days*, ed. Norbert Samuelson and David Novak, pp. 185–213; Norbert Samuelson, "Maimonides' Doctrine of Creation," *Harvard Theological Review* 84 (1991): 249–71.

[11] Here, as elsewhere, I follow Cornford's translation.

Unlike Genesis, the *Timaeus* contains numerous qualifications about the subject it addresses and the degree of precision it can bring to bear. At 29d, it says that it will offer a likely story (*eikos muthos*), rather than a scientific account, a warning that is repeated numerous times throughout the dialogue.[12] I take this to mean (1) that it will aim at the most probable account rather than one that is known to be true and (2) that the reader should not expect consistency on all points. One point on which people have accused Plato of inconsistency is his account of the creation of time. As we saw, the dialogue asserts that time was created along with the heavens (37e–38b). Not only did day and night come to be, but temporal designations such as *was* and *shall be* did as well. On the other hand, the dialogue goes into detail about what the Demiurge did "before" time was created (31b–36e) and even more detail about disorderly motion in the receptacle "before" order is imposed. According to 48b: "We must, in fact, consider in itself the nature of fire and water, air and earth, before the generation of the Heaven, and their condition before Heaven was."[13] How can there be events of any sort before the creation of time?

Nor is that all. According to the narrative of the *Timaeus*, body is produced before soul, even though, as the narrator eventually admits (34c), this order is a concession to human fallibility and

---

[12] For example 44d, 48d, 53d, 55d, 56a, 57d, 59c, 68d. Needless to say, the significance of *eikos muthos* has been the subject of endless debate. For a recent discussion, see Donald J. Zeyl's introductory essay to the *Timaeus*, pp. xx–xxxiii. According to Zeyl, the distinction between an account that is and is not perfectly consistent and accurate is not the same as the distinction between a literal account and a metaphorical one. This is true if one is speaking in principle. The problem is that the dialogue is *both* a likely story *and* one that contains a large number of metaphors. So it is far from clear that Plato is thinking of Zeyl's distinction in this passage. One problem with metaphor is its lack of precision. Another problem is that the connotations of one metaphor, for example, the comparison between the receptacle and a mass of gold, may be inconsistent with those of another, for example, the comparison between the receptacle and a winnowing basket. So the issue, as Zeyl himself comes to see, is not just probability but obscurity.

[13] Cf. *Timaeus* 52d.

cannot be the true one. In regard to the Demiurge, we are warned (28c) that it is difficult to identify the maker and father of all things and that even if we could, we cannot speak of him to all of humanity. Given Maimonides' repeated warnings about the impossibility of expressing himself in simple, expository form and the fact that he takes the first six days of creation metaphorically, one might have expected him to feel at home with the *Timaeus* and to recognize that no narrative account of the origin of the world can be taken literally.[14] We saw, however, that this is not the case.

## II

Of the various strategies for interpreting the *Timaeus*, the dominant one among Platonists in antiquity was to argue that the creation narrative should not be taken literally but viewed as a teaching device analogous to a mathematical demonstration – in short, something that uses temporal order to represent logical order.[15] Just as Plato describes the origin of the ideal state in the *Republic* in a historical fashion, beginning with a primitive society and adding levels of complexity, it was argued that he does the same thing with the origin of the world in the *Timaeus*. In neither case is there reason to suppose that he is committed to a particular sequence of events – or any sequence.

Aristotle rejects this interpretation on the grounds that the analogy with a mathematical demonstration does not hold.[16] In a demonstration, the conclusion follows directly from the premises.

---

[14] See, for example, *GP* Introduction, pp. 6–8.

[15] *De Caelo* 279b32–280a11. For a discussion of this tradition, see A. E. Taylor, *A Commentary on Plato's Timaeus*, pp. 66–69, as well as Matthias Baltes, *Die Weltentstehung des Platonischen Timaios nach den Antiken Interpreten*, Vol. 1; and J. F. Phillips, "NeoPlatonic Exegeses of Plato's Cosmology," *Journal of the History of Philosophy* 35 (1997): 173–97. The main dissenters are Philo (*On the Eternity of the World*, 13–16), Plutarch (*On the Creation of the Soul in the Timaeus*, 1013e), and Atticus. Proclus mentions Plutarch and Atticus in his *Commentary on the Timaeus* at 84f (Diehl, Vol. 1, pp. 232–33).

[16] Ibid.

But according to Plato's account in the *Timaeus*, one state (order) arises out of a contrary one (disorder), which is impossible without an interval of time to separate them. As Harold Cherniss remarks, this objection constitutes a *petitio principii* because it assumes that the production of order from disorder is, in fact, a temporal process – precisely the point at issue.[17] One suspects that Aristotle adopted a literal interpretation to distance himself from Plato on what he (Aristotle) considers the fundamental issue: that it is impossible for something that is generated to exist forever. For those who accept the metaphorical reading, this point can be taken in stride, because for them the *Timaeus* is not talking about temporal generation at all.

The crux of the metaphorical interpretation concerns the meaning of *genesis* and its derivatives. Obviously, it can refer to a temporal beginning, in which case images such as *father, mother,* and *maker* are appropriate. In a Platonic context, however, it can also refer to the instability of the sensible world. Cornford translates *Timaeus* 27d as:

> We must, then, in my judgment, first make this distinction: what is that which is always real and has no becoming, and what is that which is *always* [my emphasis] becoming and is never real?[18]

To stay with Cornford, if we are talking about an ongoing process of change, individual things will come to be and pass away, but the process itself can go on forever. If this is what Plato means, images such as father, mother, and maker are misleading because the cause is not something that produces offspring at a given moment but something that sustains the coming to be and passing away of sensible things eternally.

[17] Cherniss, *Aristotle's Criticism of Plato and the Academy*, pp. 421–22.
[18] *Plato's Cosmology*, p. 22.

Again the problem has to do with metaphor. When does Plato use it, and what is he trying communicate by doing so? He is too good a writer to say, "Be careful: the following passage may contain nonliteral discourse and confuse unsuspecting readers." Consider the way he introduces the main topic of the dialogue at 27c:

> We who are now to discourse about the world – how it came into being, or perhaps had no beginning of existence...

And at 28b:

> Has it always [*aëi*] been, without any source of becoming; or has it come to be [*gegonen*], starting from some beginning? It has come to be; for it can be seen and touched and has body, and all such things are sensible; and, as we saw, sensible things, that are to be apprehended by belief together with sensation, are things that become [*gignomena*] and can be generated [*genneta*].

As Richard Sorabji points out, those who prefer the literal interpretation can interpret these passages in a straightforward way: Plato raises the question of eternity or creation and comes down on the side of the latter.[19]

For those who prefer the metaphorical interpretation, the question is not so simple. The middle Platonist Calvenus Taurus distinguishes four senses of generation. A thing is generated if (1) it is of the same genus as what is generated, (2) it is composite even if in fact it has never been combined, (3) it is forever in the process of being generated, and (4) it is dependent for its existence on an external source.[20] In regard to (4), Taurus points out that

---

[19] *TCC*, p. 275.

[20] These senses are recorded by Philoponus, *On the Eternity of the World* 6.8 (ed. Rabe, p. 145). Cf. Proclus, *Commentary on the Timaeus* 85f (Diehl, Vol. 1, p. 279). Obviously the meanings are not mutually exclusive: something that is composite can (in fact, usually is) in flux and depends for its existence on something else. For Proclus' reliance on more than one meaning, see J. F. Phillips, "Neoplatonic Exegeses of Plato's Cosmology," *Journal of the History of Philosophy* 35 (1997): 180–82. Also note Maimonides' Assumption 21 for proving the existence of God (*GP* 2, Introduction, p. 238): "Everything that is composed of two notions has necessarily that composition

even those who believe the world is eternal would admit that the moon possesses generated light from the sun. Plotinus expresses the same sentiment, saying that things are generated if they are eternally derived from something else.[21] In a more general way, Proclus maintains in his commentary on the *Timaeus* that something should be deemed *generated* if it does not possess the whole of its essence or energy as one unified thing.[22] It is from this tradition that we get the idea of the eternal generation of the world from a simple, immaterial source. By the time Maimonides wrote the *Guide*, eternal generation was an established part of the philosophic scene as shown by the fact that he attributes it even to thinkers in the Aristotelian tradition.[23]

If Taurus is right about Plato's use of "comes to be" in the earlier passage, the issue is not temporal creation versus eternity but eternal dependence on God versus eternal self-subsistence. Consider the argument that follows: (1) the world is corporeal and is apprehended by sensation and belief, (2) all such things are in process of becoming and can be generated, (3) that which becomes does so by virtue of a cause.[24] The narrator concludes that the world has a cause and identifies it as the maker and father of all things. Students of medieval philosophy will recognize that this argument resembles later *Kalām* arguments for the existence of God, because it moves from the origin of the world to God rather than vice versa. Unfortunately, the argument is too abbreviated to know what the narrator means. He could be saying that all corporeal things have a history that includes a temporal beginning or that all corporeal

as the cause of its existence as it really is, and consequently is not necessarily existent in respect to its own essence, for it exists in virtue of the existence of its two parts and of their composition." In short, everything that is composite is derivative.

[21] *EN* 2.4.5.24, cf. 2.9.3.11. Cf. *GP* 2.21, p. 315.

[22] Proclus, *Commentary on the Timaeus* 85b (Diehl, Vol. 1, p. 277).

[23] *GP* 2.21, p. 316.

[24] Gregory Vlastos, "Creation in the 'Timaeus': Is It a Fiction?" in *Studies in Plato's Metaphysics*, ed. R. E. Allen, p. 402: objects that *genneta* should not be rendered "can be generated" but "have been generated." More on Vlastos later.

things occupy a lower order of existence from forms and are in a state of perpetual flux. On the surface, neither claim is unreasonable – nor for that matter are they incompatible.

In addition to Cherniss and Cornford, Zeller, Taylor, and Frutiger also defend the metaphorical reading.[25] One advantage is that it connects the *Timaeus* with other dialogues in which Plato contrasts the worlds of being and becoming in a context in which the temporal origin of the latter is not at issue.[26] If the metaphorical reading is true, the Demiurge must also be viewed as a literary device for driving home a philosophic point: that the world of becoming occupies an intermediate state between complete order and complete chaos and can be understood as the product of Reason and Necessity. According to the Neoplatonic reading, to the degree that it is the product of two forces, it is generated. This does not mean that Reason and Necessity actually join together or that a creating God shapes and bends raw materials but that the two forces are logically prior to the world of becoming and together explain its status: an image that strives to be like an eternal model but falls short.

The metaphorical interpretation is challenged by Hackforth and Vlastos, in part because the argument of 28b–c seems to contain no evidence of metaphor.[27] In Vlastos's words:

> No metaphorical or figurative language infiltrates this sequence of propositions. *Eikos muthos* is not even mentioned until later (29d 2). And metaphor does not enter the texture of Timaeus' discourse until the reference to the 'Maker and Father of this world,' i.e. until after the generation of the world has been proved.

---

[25] Eduard Zeller, *Plato and the Older Academy*, pp. 363–68; Taylor, *A Commentary*, pp. 66–69; Frutiger, *Les mythes de Platon*, pp. 199–209.

[26] See, for example, *Republic* 518c, 521d; *Theaetetus* 152d; *Sophist* 248a.

[27] R. Hackforth, "Plato's Cosmogony," *Classical Quarterly* N.S. 9 (1959): 17–22; and Vlastos, "Creation," pp. 402–4. Hackforth and Vlastos have something of an ally in Sorabji, *TCC*, pp. 272–75.

Although it is true that "maker and father" does not appear until after the generation of the world has been proved, Vlastos neglects to mention that it appears *directly* after. The price he pays for this reading is that the argument of 28b–c is isolated from the rest of the dialogue, not to mention the many discussions of being and becoming in other dialogues. If Vlastos is right, Plato would have to shift gears immediately after stating the argument, moving from what Vlastos calls "firm metaphysical doctrine" to a likely story not consistent on all points. Nothing in the text indicates that such a radical transition has been made.

What about the motion prior to the creation of the heavens, when, we are told, time begins? A proponent of the metaphorical interpretation would say that all temporal references should be taken as claims of ontological priority. If there are disorderly motions in the receptacle before Reason persuades Necessity, all this means is that without Reason, we would have no regular motion and thus no time, not that there was a period in which motion was chaotic and could not be measured. According to the literal interpretation, that is exactly what Plato did mean: a period of disorderly motion and therefore chaotic time preceded the creation of orderly motion and measured time. Thus, Vlastos argues that to say that the Demiurge introduced *measurable* time flow is not to say that he introduced time flow as such.[28] To take his example, suppose A, B, and C are successive instants but that we have no way of telling whether the interval AB is longer, shorter, or equal to BC. In this case, we would have temporal succession but not temporal measure.

There is no conceptual problem in saying that succession of this sort occurs in the absence of measurable time. The question is whether Plato was aware of the distinction and wrote this part of the

[28] Vlastos, "Creation," p. 410.

46

*Timaeus* to call attention to it. Recall, as Vlastos does, that according to 37e, *was* and *shall be* (past and future) come to be with the creation of the heavens.[29] Without past and future, we do not have temporal passage in any sense. As Vlastos admits, temporal succession without measure *does* exhibit structure to the degree that it is a transitive, asymmetrical, irreflexive continuum, something about which one could make rational inferences and develop a logic. Surely this is more than Plato would have been willing to attribute to the chaotic motion of the sensible world prior to the imposition of order by Reason. Again from Vlastos: "The material world would have been orderless were it not ordered by a designing Mind."[30] So, plausible as it might be, the distinction between temporal succession and temporal measure does not fit the *Timaeus*' description of chaos and thus cannot be ascribed to Plato without making a conceptual leap.

There is also the problem of how to account for the vestiges of earth, air, fire, and water that shake and are shaken by the receptacle before the creation of time. Recall the argument that things apprehended by sense are in the process of becoming and that what becomes does so by virtue of a cause. Two passages suggest that these things must be regarded as sensible. The first is 30a, where the narrator says that the Demiurge took over "all that is visible" and in chaotic motion and brought it from disorder to order. The second is the description of the receptacle at 52d–e: "Now the nurse of Becoming, being made watery and fiery and receiving the characters of earth and air, and qualified by all the other affections that go with these, had every sort of diverse appearance

---

[29] According to Vlastos, "Creation," pp. 411–12, to say that past and future come into existence when time does is not to say that they come into existence *only* when time does. But then the Demiurge does not really *create* past and future, he just provides another period in which they apply. This is very difficult to reconcile with the text.

[30] Ibid.

to the sight." The most natural interpretation is that whatever it lacked in the way of structure, the primordial chaos was visible.[31] Does this mean that it is the product of another creation prior to the creation of time? If so, what cause was responsible for it, and how did that cause operate?

The dialogue says nothing about this issue, nor could it without introducing a second Demiurge or a previous act of creation by the original Demiurge, neither of which has any textual support. The alternative is to say that there were no events of any sort prior to the creation of time because there was no "creation" in the normal sense of the term: all Plato is trying to teach us is that whatever order the world exhibits is due to Reason, not to the effects of mechanical processes like cooling and heating, condensation and rarefaction, and the like. As the narrator says (46d), "Such things are incapable of any plan or intelligence for any purpose." As we saw, there is no order without a designing mind.

Given the imprecision of the text, both the literal and the metaphorical interpretation are possible. It is even possible that Plato wrote the dialogue with this ambiguity in mind or that, as John Dillon argues, the dialogue contains problems that Plato himself declined to solve.[32] One of its main contentions is that when we deal with the sensible world, the line between literal truth and speculation is hard to discern. In view of the flux to which sensible things are subject, our attempts to identify earth, air, fire, and water as elements – even our ability to say *this* or *that* in reference to them – is suspect.[33] Although people talk as if they knew what these

---

[31] Needless to say, Vlastos, "Creation," pp. 403–405, denies this on the grounds that the reference to vision at 30a is not to be taken seriously. His point is in answer to Zeller, *Plato and the Older Academy*, p. 365.

[32] John Dillon, *The Middle Platonists*, p. 6.

[33] *Timaeus* 47e–48a, 49a–50a.

things are and how they came to be, the narrator assures us that (48b) "to this day no one has explained their generation." Note, however, that instead of following this remark by saying, "Here then is the real truth of the matter," the narrator launches into another warning about the difficulty of the subject. Looking at the dialogue as a whole, all we know for certain is that there are two orders of reality, being and becoming, and that behind everything we experience is a rational principle working for good ends. Beyond that, neither the dialogue nor the subject permits more than educated guesses.

From the perspective of Maimonides, both the literal and the metaphorical interpretations play an important role. We will see that, according to him, Plato believed that although the order or structure of the world was created *de novo*, its material component is eternal. He therefore takes Plato to hold that the material component of the world proceeds from God in a timeless fashion. This enables him to say that Plato believed in a God who organizes things for a purpose. As noted earlier, the metaphorical interpretation also finds its way into his view of Aristotle. Thus (*GP* 2.21, p. 316): "When he [Aristotle or an Aristotelian philosopher] says that the first intelligence proceeds from God . . . it is clear that he does not wish to signify thereby that first a certain thing was, and then, later, the thing necessarily proceeding from the first thing was produced in time." This is the crux of the theory of emanation as articulated by Plotinus and taken up and transformed by Alfarabi and Avicenna. We will also see that the differences between the literal and metaphorical interpretation are more than temporal because, according to Maimonides, purpose and particularization require that something not exist and then be brought into existence for a desired end. By denying that there was a first moment in time, the metaphorical interpretation is incompatible with free will in God – at least as Maimonides understands it.

### III

In addition to the question of creation, there is the question of matter. At *GP* 2.13 (p. 283), Maimonides claims that the philosophers reject creation *ex nihilo* on the grounds that it is impossible to bring something into existence from nothing at all. The difference between Plato and Aristotle is that the former believes that God imposed form on preexistent matter in the first instant of time while the latter believes that the information of matter is eternal and continuous. This overlooks the fact that the natural philosophy of the *Timaeus* is different from that of Aristotle's *Physics*. As Cornford indicates, Plato never refers to the receptacle as *matter*.[34] In fact, the receptacle is not even called a body but rather that which receives bodies (50b). By the same token, it is not that *out of which* things are made but that *in which* images of the forms appear and from which they perish. The difference is significant.

For Aristotle, matter *is* that out of which things come to be. Matter is changed by virtue of the fact that what was potential becomes actual: the bronze that is shapeless becomes a statue, the person who cannot play a note becomes musical. This is exactly what the *Timaeus* denies in regard to the receptacle. The picture is complicated by the fact that the narrator goes on to compare the receptacle to a mass of gold at 50a–c. This passage is notoriously difficult. It could suggest, as it did to Aristotle, that the receptacle is a substratum from which corporeal things are generated: "He [Plato] says, indeed, that it is a substratum prior to the so-called 'elements' – underlying them, as gold underlies the things that are fashioned from gold."[35] Yet this cannot be true, because we are told at 50b–c that the receptacle "never in any way whatsoever takes on

---

[34] *Plato's Cosmology*, p. 181. Others who make this point include Taylor, *Commentary* (on 52b); and Cherniss, *Aristotle's Criticism*, pp. 83–173.

[35] Aristotle, *On Generation and Corruption*, 329a13–24. Compare this passage to *Physics* 209a11, where Aristotle claims that in the *Timaeus*, Plato identified matter with space.

any character that is like any of the things that enter it."[36] Rather than introduce the concept of a substratum, the point of the analogy is to say that just as gold is indifferent to the shape it is in and can receive any shape at all, the receptacle is indifferent to the qualities that pass through it. According to 50b: "It must be called always the same; for it never departs at all from its own character."

Unlike a substratum, the receptacle does not *become* hot, cold, wet, or dry and thus cannot be viewed as a subject of change. Neither does it go from potency to act. Rather the receptacle is quality neutral, or else when opposite qualities entered it, it would not receive one as easily as it does the other. This would make it impossible for it to serve as a universal matrix (*ekmageion*) for sensible qualities. Thus, 50e: "That which is to receive in itself all kinds must be free from all characters; just like the base which the makers of scented ointments skillfully contrive to start with." And 51a: "The mother and Receptacle of what has come to be visible and otherwise sensible must not be called earth or air or fire or water, nor any of their compounds or components."

Instead of comparing the receptacle to a mass of gold or a female parent, it would be better to follow Plotinus and compare it to a mirror in which qualities are reflected temporarily but cause no underlying change in the medium of reflection.[37] This comparison, too, is imperfect, because a mirror can be seen in its own right whereas the receptacle cannot; but at least it allows us to see that the receptacle is unaffected by the things that pass through it. According to 51b, we will not be wrong if we call the receptacle invisible, characterless, all receiving, and "partaking in some very puzzling way of the intelligible." As to what the nature of this participation is, we do not know, except that the receptacle, which is

---

[36] Plato does not help matters by saying at 50c that the receptacle is changed and diversified by the things that enter it. Fortunately this remark is qualified in the next line: it *appears* [Cornford's emphasis] to have different qualities at different times.

[37] *EN* 3.6.14.

later identified with space, is not apprehended by the mind or the senses but by a bastard reason.

The identification of the receptacle with space occurs at 52a along with the claim that space is eternal and indestructible. In view of the question Plato raises at 28b (Has it always been, without any source of becoming, or has it come to be?), I take the argument of 52a to imply that space has no source: it is simply a given of the world as we know it. When the narrator says at 30a that the Demiurge took over all that is visible and brought it from disorder to order, he is referring to the images in the receptacle, not to the receptacle itself.

For a monotheist like Maimonides, this poses a problem. If space is eternal and there is no cause of its existence, then according to the argument Proclus used against Aristotle, it would have to be able to sustain itself in existence for all time. To do this, it would have to possess infinite power and thus be infinite itself. This is clearly impossible given the view that the world is finite. If the receptacle cannot sustain itself, the only thing that can sustain it is God. There is, however, no evidence that Plato looked at the matter this way. He takes it as obvious that the world contains a spatial dimension and nowhere says that the Demiurge is responsible for creating it or even for setting it in motion. All the Demiurge does is organize the images that pass through it by giving them a distinct configuration according to shape and number.

The *Timaeus* makes a fresh start at 52a–b by claiming that there are three factors responsible for the world: forms, images of the forms, and the space in which the images appear. To this we may add the Demiurge himself. Cornford objects that because the two parents of becoming, the form and the receptacle, are both eternal and unchanging, there is no way for an image cast by a form to be inconstant and fleeting.[38] The standard Platonic doctrine is that all

[38] Cornford, *Plato's Cosmology*, p. 196.

motion derives from soul, which is defined as self-moving motion.[39] The question is whether that doctrine can be extended to include the disorderly motion of the receptacle prior to the imposition of order by Reason. According to 53a, not only are the contents of the receptacle in motion but so, too, is the receptacle itself. Some have argued that this motion is purely mechanical, some have posited an evil world soul that stands in opposition to the good one, while others have posited an irrational element in the world soul itself.[40] Once again the dialogue leaves us guessing.

For my purposes, the most serious problem is not the disorderly motion of the images in the receptacle, but the fact that there are images at all. Like space, forms are ungenerated and indestructible; unlike space, they do not receive anything into themselves or enter into anything else. How, then, can Plato say that forms cast or throw off reflections in a spatial medium? Again, he is speaking metaphorically. But what is the language of image and reflection a metaphor for? How exactly does the form produce an image of itself? At 50c, the narrator says that images are "impressions" taken from the forms "in a strange manner that is hard to express." The problem is that, left to their own devices, forms are not efficient causes and do not explain the existence of what participates in them. That is the job of the Demiurge. But the Demiurge is of no help on this issue because he does not create the "traces" of earth, air, fire, and water in the receptacle; all he does is impose order on them. To the degree that they are traces of anything, they must already participate in some form or another, albeit imperfectly. The problem is that nothing in the *Timaeus* allows us to say how they get on the scene in the first place.

In hindsight, one can imagine invoking the doctrine of emanation to explain the causal efficacy of forms, but at this juncture

---

[39] *Phaedrus* 245c–246a; *Laws* 894b–896c.
[40] See Ulrich Wilamowitz-Moellendorf, *Platon* II, pp. 320–21; and Cornford, *Plato's Cosmology*, pp. 209–10.

no such doctrine is available: all we have are visual metaphors applied to a nonvisual subject. I submit that Plato does not resolve the question of how images are produced because he never raised it. Forms and space are eternal and require no explanation. Experience indicates that reflections of the forms appear in space and eventually pass out of it. These are the factors needed to explain the material world, and any attempt to derive them from something more fundamental is outside the scope of Platonic philosophy. Much the same is true of the Demiurge. He is needed to account for how order emerges from disorder. Within the confines of the dialogue, any attempt to ask from where he comes or from what he derives his authority is misplaced. As with Aristotle, Plato is concerned with the structure of the world, not its origin.

IV

Maimonides' description of the Platonic view of creation runs as follows (*GP* 2.13, p. 283):

> They [the followers of Plato] believe that there exists a certain matter that is eternal as the deity is eternal; and that He does not exist without it, nor does it exist without Him. They do not believe that it has the same rank in what exists as He . . . but that He is the cause of its existence; and that it has the same relation toward Him as, for instance, clay has toward a potter or iron toward a smith; and that He creates in it whatever He wishes. Thus He sometimes forms out of it a heaven and an earth, and sometimes He forms out of it something else.

In short, matter is eternal. Although different forms may enter it or pass away, it is not subject to generation or destruction itself. To say that matter does not have the same rank as God is to say that although it is coeternal with God, without God's decision to impose form, it would lack any positive determination.[41]

Note, however, that even though matter is eternal, according to Maimonides' account, God is still the cause of its existence. This can only refer to eternal generation. If so, God's contribution is twofold: first to sustain matter in existence and then to give it an identity as heavenly matter, earthly matter, or something else. Whereas the former goes on forever, the latter occurs *de novo*. If this is true, creation would resemble the way a craftsman imposes form on matter, exactly the way Maimonides characterizes the Platonic view. Because the order and structure of the world is created, according to Maimonides, it must eventually perish, in which case the world will return to the material chaos from which it came. This raises the possibility that there can be a second imposition of form and thus a succession of worlds beyond this one.[42]

After distinguishing the Platonic from the Aristotelian position at *GP* 2.13, Maimonides says something peculiar: because the Platonists believe in eternity, there is no difference between the Platonic view and the Aristotelian one. This remark seems to conflict with *GP* 2.25, where, after rejecting the Aristotelian view, he says that the Platonic one is acceptable because it accepts miracles and upholds the foundation of the Law. The difference can be explained as follows. If one wishes to emphasize creation *ex nihilo*, there is no real difference between the views of Plato and Aristotle because they both believe in the eternity of matter. If, however, one

[41] Note that Maimonides takes the mention of white sapphire stones under the feet of God at Exodus 24.10 to be a reference to the transparency and indeterminacy of prime matter. Thus (*GP* 1.28, pp. 60–61): "For what they [Moses, Aaron, and the elders of Israel] apprehended was the true reality of first matter, which derives from Him . . . He being the cause of its existence." Cf. 2.26, p. 331, where Maimonides takes Exodus 24.10 as a reference to earthly matter.

[42] According to Wolfson, *Studies*, Vol. 1, p. 240, this possibility derives from *De Caelo* 279b12–13, where Aristotle attributes the infinite succession view to Empedocles and Heraclitus. For Maimonides' rejection of successive worlds, see *GP* 2.30, p. 349.

wishes to emphasize creation *de novo*, the Platonic view resembles the biblical one because it upholds the creation of the cosmos. By affirming creation *de novo* and rejecting creation *ex nihilo*, the Platonic view serves an important dialectical function by providing a middle ground between Aristotle, who rejects creation *de novo*, and the Bible, which, in Maimonides' opinion, accepts both.

Again dialectical functions do not always comport with historical facts. If the receptacle is not a subject of change, it is misleading to say that God shapes it as a potter shapes clay. Recall, however, that Maimonides' knowledge of Plato is derived from Aristotle. Given Aristotle's claim that the purpose of the gold analogy is to introduce the concept of a material substratum, Maimonides' view is to be expected. To bring the world from disorder to order is to take a formless material and give it shape.[43] In effect, Maimonides commits Plato to two kinds of matter: a prime matter that is coeternal with God and a matter that has received the form of a heavenly or earthly element.[44]

Aside from reliance on Aristotle, there is another reason why Maimonides' view of Plato is forced. The *Timaeus* is not committed to monotheism. Instead of an all-powerful being who commands things into existence, the Demiurge made the world "as excellent and perfect as possible."[45] As we saw, the *Timaeus* assumes that certain features of the world are given, so there is no need to seek an explanation for them. This will be corrected once the concept of emanation is worked out, but that took centuries to develop. From Maimonides' perspective, the suggestion that there are features of the world that require no explanation poses a problem. Apart from God, nothing is given, which is a way of saying that everything depends for its existence on God or is generated by God. Whether

[43] See n. 23.
[44] For further exposition on prime matter, see *GP* 2.17, p. 297.
[45] *Timaeus* 30b.

it is generated eternally or *de novo* is another issue; the important point is that it is generated at all.

Unlike a modern historian of philosophy, who is obliged to point out that the *Timaeus* is not dealing with a necessary being as medieval philosophers understood the term, Maimonides ignores this fact or adopts an interpretative stance from which it becomes unimportant. Note, for example, that when he begins his discussion of creation at *GP* 2.13, he does so by saying that he will only consider the views of "those who believe that there is an existent deity." All the views he discusses take God to be the source of all existence and thus more than a Demiurge. Where they disagree is on how God is the source.

From Maimonides' perspective, the Demiurge as described in the *Timaeus* is not a deity but a throwback to mythology. That is why he affirms, contrary to the text of the *Timaeus*, that the Platonic view of creation holds that God is the cause of matter – not because Plato said it but because in Maimonides' opinion, his view would not be worth considering unless he believed it. To someone who thinks there is one source for everything, even if matter is an eternal feature of the world, it still needs a cause. As we will see, Maimonides is closer to the truth if we shift from Platonism proper to Neoplatonism, because Plotinus did believe in a common source for all things. The fact remains, however, that the historical Plato is comfortable with ontological givens and a Demiurge who strives to overcome the limits they impose. He is also comfortable with two forces, Reason and Necessity, rather than one. Once we put everything in the hands of a single source, the way is open to claim that the eternal generation of prime matter is distinct from the temporal creation of heaven and earth – exactly what Maimonides' characterization of Plato maintains.

Although Maimonides makes clear that he does not prefer the Platonic view of creation (*GP* 2.13, p. 283), we saw that he thinks it is compatible with free will in God and can be supported by passages where the Demiurge is said to deliberate, make judgments, and promise not to destroy the heavens. A God with free will is more than a first cause of the world but a God who can give the gift of existence, issue commandments, and promise redemption. It could be said, therefore, that unless God exercises free will, the biblical worldview would collapse. That is why Maimonides thinks belief in creation is a pillar of the Law and eternal emanation a threat.

This is all a way of saying that with the idea of an infinite God, the question of origin is unavoidable. Because infinity has no limits, nothing escapes the infinite. Once we say that God is infinite, everything is either God or an offspring of God. For essentialists like Plato and Aristotle, infinity is not a mark of perfection. To have an essence is to have a limit, to be one thing rather than another. As Plato says of the forms, each one is *monoëidēs*.[46] The unlimited or indefinite is the mark of what lacks essence and defies understanding. For Plato, this applies to the appearances of earth, air, fire, and water in the receptacle, things so caught up in the flux of the sensible realm that they never appear as the same thing over time and cannot even be called *this* (49b–d). For Aristotle, too, perfection means finitude or the embodiment of form.[47] In both cases anything that is comprehensible must fall under a description or manifest a discernible quality.

For Maimonides, this is not true. Again, following in the footsteps of the Neoplatonists, Maimonides believes that the God who has no limits also has no discernible essence.[48] Thus, *GP* 1.50 (p. 111): "You must know that He ... has in no way and in no mode any essential attribute ... "; and 1.52 (p. 115): "He ... has no causes anterior to Him that are the cause of His existence and by which, in consequence, He is defined. For this reason it is well known among

[46] *Phaedo* 78d, 80b, 83e.
[47] Cf. Joseph Owens, *The Doctrine of Being*, p. 468.
[48] On this point, see the *Liber de Causis*, 8–9.

all people engaged in speculation . . . that God cannot be defined." Nothing is independent of this God or can resist the force of his decrees. So certain is Maimonides of this that he cannot imagine how a serious thinker could fail to accept it.

We may conclude that even if Maimonides read the whole *Timaeus*, he would have had no patience with the idea of a Demiurge. Instead he interprets Plato as saying that God is both the cause of matter and the agent who imposes shape or form on it. How philosophy progressed from the essentialism of Plato and Aristotle to the anti-essentialism of Maimonides, and more specifically, how the central question of philosophy became the origin of the world and not its structure, remains to be seen.

# 3

# Aristotle and the Arguments for Eternity

ACCORDING TO MAIMONIDES, ARISTOTLE BELIEVED THAT the world is eternal and that it has always existed in the form in which it now exists. As Davidson remarks, the latter claim is important because Maimonides' rendering of the Platonic view is that although the material component of the world is eternal, its form or structure was imposed by God during creation.[1] This is why the Platonic view leaves room for divine volition. The Aristotelian view does not because it denies both creation *ex nihilo* and the creation of the cosmos *de novo*. In the words of Maimonides (*GP* 2.12, p. 284): "He [Aristotle] thinks that this being as a whole, such as it is, has never ceased to be and will never do so; that the permanent thing

[1] *PEC*, pp. 9–10.

not subject to generation and passing-away, namely the heaven, likewise does not cease to be; that time and motion are perpetual and everlasting and not subject to generation and passing-away; and also that the thing subject to generation and passing-away, namely, that which is beneath the sphere of the moon, does not cease to be." As such, the Aristotelian position understands creation as eternal dependence on God and constitutes the extreme opposite of the Mosaic.[2]

The crux of this position is a principle articulated throughout the Aristotelian corpus: anything that is eternal is necessary.[3] If the present form of the world always was and always will be, it is necessary and no other form is possible. Thus (ibid.): "No innovation can take place in it that is not according to its nature." This means that any changes that occur are local and do not affect the overall structure of the world. So described, the Aristotelian position leaves no room for free choice. But after saying that no innovation can take place, Maimonides goes on to assert something that appears anomalous: according to Aristotle, "All that exists has been brought into existence, in the state in which it is at present, by God through His volition."

If the present form of the world is necessary, how can it be brought into existence by divine volition? Maimonides concedes

---

[2] Both Harvey ("Maimonides' Puzzle" p. 77) and Abraham Nuriel ("The Question of a Primordial or Created World in the Philosophy of Maimonides" (in Hebrew), *Tarbiz* 33 [1964]: 372–87) point out that Maimonides sometimes uses *al-bāri'* (the creator) in a manner that is consistent with the Aristotelian view of creation, for example, 2.14, p. 288; 2.19, p. 302. This should not surprise us. According to Maimonides, the Aristotelian view is a reasonable position and does account for the emergence of the world from God. But it does not follow that it represents Maimonides' preferred view. In most cases, *al-bāri'* is neutral with respect to creation and eternity and serves only as another name for God. Cf. *MT* 1, Basic Principles of the Torah, 1.7, 2.8. In response to Nuriel, see Aviezer Ravitzky, "The Question of a Created or Primordial World in the Philosophy of Maimonides," (in Hebrew), *Tarbiz* 35 (1966): 333–48.

[3] *On Generation and Corruption* 338a1–4; *Physics* 203b 29; *Metaphysics* 1050b8–15.

that he is not talking about Aristotle's view as expressed in the text but "what his opinion comes to." Avicenna refers to an eternal will, and as discussed in the next chapter, Plotinus ascribes will to the first principle, albeit in a context that allows for reduced standards of rigor.[4] If God wills the existence of the world, and God's will does not change, the world cannot change either. By contrast Maimonides argues (*GP* 2.18) that a will that cannot change or will and not will is not really a will at all. Later (2.21) he claims that people who ascribe will to a being who cannot change are playing with words. So although the Aristotelians may attribute will to God, Davidson is right to say that in Maimonides' opinion, they are using *will* in a Pickwickian sense.[5] Note, for example, that Maimonides concludes his presentation of the Aristotelian position by saying that it offers us a deity in whom "it is impossible that a volition should undergo a change . . . or a new will arise in Him." As applied to Genesis 1, this means that creation is nothing but the eternal generation of the world from God.

As with Plato, Maimonides' view of Aristotle is more thematic than historical. We saw that Aristotle's God explains the eternal motion of the heavens, not their existence. At no point does Aristotle suggest that either is the product of volition. But he does argue for the eternity of the world, and this is what interests Maimonides. At *GP* 2.14–15, Maimonides distinguishes between arguments for eternity that derive from the nature of the world and arguments that derive from the nature of God. It is to these arguments that we now turn. In the interest of simplicity, I follow the order in which Maimonides presents them.

---

[4] Avicenna, *Al-Shifā'* (*The Metaphysics Healing*) 8.7, pp. 366–67. For the attribution of voluntarism to Plotinus, see Chapter 4, n. 54.

[5] *PEC*, p. 2, n. 3. Contrast Harvey ("Maimonides' Puzzle," *M*, pp. 77–78), who thinks that if both Aristotle and Maimonides accept God's necessity and both speak of divine will, "on the allegedly crucial question of divine necessity and divine will there is no evident difference between Aristotle and Maimonides."

I

The first proof for eternity that derives from the nature of the world occurs at *Physics* 8.1 and concerns the eternity of motion. In essence, it tries to show that if there were a first motion, there would have to be motion prior to that motion, so that the idea of a first motion is absurd. To understand what Maimonides is getting at, it is helpful to recognize that throughout much of the *Physics*, Aristotle treats motion (*kinēsis*) and change (*metabolē*) as synonyms.[6] As Maimonides puts it (*GP* 2. Introduction, Premise 5): "Every motion is a change and transition from potentiality to actuality." According to the usual account, change occurs in one of four categories: (1) substance, which involves coming to be and passing away; (2) quality, which involves alteration; (3) quantity, which involves growth and diminution; and (4) place, which involves locomotion.[7]

No matter what category we are talking about, motion requires the presence of an agent and a patient. Before there can be cutting, there must be something capable of being cut. If there were a first motion, either agent and patient would have to have a beginning, or both would have to be eternal. Suppose they had a beginning. In that case there must be motion prior to the first motion, namely, the action by which agent and patient were brought into existence. If there is motion before the first motion, the idea of a first motion makes no sense. Following Averroes, Davidson objects that Aristotle fails to explain why the coming into existence of the physical world cannot be the first motion.[8] In this case, motion and the physical world would come to be at the same time. The objection is valid if

---

[6] *Physics* 201a2, 201a7, 201b18.

[7] *Physics* 200b32–34, 201a10–14, 223a29–34. Cf. *GP* 2. Introduction, Premise 4.

[8] *PEC*, p. 18. Averroes' solution is to say that according to Aristotle, motion in place is the primary form of motion, so that the coming into existence of the physical world would require not just motion but motion from one place to another. In short, the physical world would already have to exist. I am not going to discuss this alternative at length for two reasons: (1) it is not part of Maimonides' treatment of creation and

we look at the argument of *Physics* 8.1 alone. If, however, we look at other parts of Aristotle's natural philosophy, including the second argument for eternity, it is not difficult to construct a reply.

We saw that coming to be and passing away qualify as motion according to the view set forth in *Physics* 3 and that this view is reiterated in Book Two of the *Guide*. Aristotle himself indicates, however, that this view is only provisional when he says at *Physics* 218b19: "We need not distinguish *at present* between motion and change." By *Physics* 5 (225a34 ff.), he maintains that motion is only a *type* of change. According to the latter view, motion involves a transition from subject to subject, as when a child grows older or an iron becomes hot. Unlike coming to be or passing away, the subject persists throughout the process. By contrast, coming to be involves a change from what is not to what is. It is impossible, Aristotle claims at *Physics* 225a25, for what is not to be in motion. "This being so," he concludes, "it follows that 'becoming' cannot be a motion: for it is that which 'is not' that 'becomes.'" By the same token, passing away is not a motion because it involves a change from what is to what is not.

As Ross points out, Aristotle is not thinking of what is not (*to mē on*) in a sense that would allow one to say that something comes from nothing.[9] According to *Physics* 191b13:

> Nothing can be said without qualification to come from what is not. But nevertheless we maintain that a thing may "come to be from what is not" – that is, in a qualified sense. For a thing comes to be from privation, which in its own nature is not-being.

In saying "it is that which is not that becomes," Aristotle means that it is that which is not *by accident*, not that which is not in itself.[10] It is still true, however, that coming to be and passing away are

(2) I argue later that for Aristotle, coming to be is not a form of motion but a form of change.

[9] Ross, *Aristotle's Physics*, p. 47.

[10] On this point, see *Physics* 225a26.

explained in terms of act and potency. When a thing comes to be, it does so not from absolutely nothing but from something that is that thing potentially. In *On Generation and Corruption* (317b16–17), he puts it this way: "Coming to be necessarily implies the preexistence of something which potentially is but actually is not, and this something is spoken of both as being and as not-being."

As long as coming to be involves a transition from potency to act, it requires an agent and a patient. In Aristotle's view, even substances come to be from a substratum that is acted on by something else. In the words of *Physics* 190b1–4: "We find in every case something that underlies from which proceeds that which comes to be; for instance, animals and plants from seed." The same would be true of the physical world if it came to be. We would have to explain how the substratum from which the world proceeded went from potency to act. Because this would require something already in action, there would have to be an action before the first action, from which it follows again that the idea of a first action is absurd.

To return to the argument at hand, the first horn of the dilemma was that agent and patient came to be. The second horn is that agent and patient are eternal and were at rest before the first motion occurred. Because rest is a privation, Aristotle seems to think it must have a cause.[11] Why would agent and patient not interact with one another? The answer is that something must prevent them from doing so. At this point Aristotle assumes either that the cause of rest must be active and therefore requires motion of its own or that removing the cause of rest constitutes motion by definition. Either way, a motion prior to the first motion is needed if the agent and patient are eternal. Because both horns of the dilemma lead to absurdity, the possibility of a first motion must be rejected.

---

[11] Why must rest have a cause? Why, that is, must agent and patient be *set* at rest? Davidson (*PEC*, p. 19) speculates that Aristotle is making an ad hoc argument against Empedocles.

The crux of Aristotle's position is that motion is not spontaneous but requires a process by which the agent comes into contact with the patient and actualizes its potential. This raises the question of what gets the process to work. Assuming that the agent and the patient are already present, what causes the former to act on the latter? Because whatever cause one gives will have to be actual rather than potential, a first motion or actualization can never be granted. Maimonides summarizes the result of both horns of the dilemma by saying (*GP* 2.14, p. 286):

> For he [Aristotle] says that if a motion is produced in time, it should be considered that everything that is produced in time is preceded by a certain motion, namely, that consisting in the passage to actuality and its being produced after it had been nonexistent. Consequently a motion exists, namely, the motion by means of which the latter motion was brought into being. Consequently the first motion must of necessity be eternal or else the series will go on to infinity.

As applied to the issue of creation, this argument makes a bold assumption: that the origin of the world is analogous to the origin of a natural thing within it.

Although Aristotle does not discuss this assumption, it is not difficult to see how he might defend it. If the origin of the world is not analogous to the origin of a natural thing within it, what is it analogous to? A composite of matter and form cannot come into existence from nothing at all. Nor is it clear on Aristotelian principles how it could come into existence from pure form. Thus, Aristotle could reply that unless the origin of the world is analogous to the origin of a natural thing within it, it would be completely mysterious.

The argument for the impossibility of a first motion is supplemented by Aristotle's view of the nature of time. As he says on several

occasions, time is the number of motion.[12] If it can be shown that
time is eternal, it would follow that motion is eternal. That time is
eternal can be inferred from the fact that time cannot exist and is
inconceivable apart from the moment, what we would call the *now*.
It is the moment that marks before and after and allows time to be
divided into units. When we count time, it is these instantaneous
units that we are counting. Without them, there would be no number and thus no time. Seen in this light, the moment is a midpoint
uniting the beginning of future time and the end of past. Because
the moment is both a beginning and an end, there must be time,
which is to say other moments, on either side of a given moment.
It follows that there can be no first or last moment and thus no first
or last motion.

Although *GP* 2.14 (p. 286) contains an oblique reference to this
argument, Maimonides never offers an explicit refutation. The reason for this may be that the argument has long been considered
arbitrary if viewed as an independent reason for accepting eternity. Even if we grant that time is composed of moments and is
inconceivable without motion, there seems to be no reason why
we cannot admit that time and motion began together in a first
moment whose boundary is a succeeding moment but not a proceeding one. As Gersonides suggests, we can use "before" in either
of two ways: one to mark a midpoint between moments of time and
one to mark a limit.[13] In all likelihood, Aristotle did not intend
this argument to stand alone but thought of it as buttressing his
argument against a first motion on metaphysical grounds. To the
degree that the metaphysical argument is vulnerable, this is as well.

The second argument for eternity has to do with matter and
is closely linked to the first. We saw that while coming to be and

---

[12] Also see *Physics* 219b2.
[13] See *WL* 6.1.21.

passing away are not forms of motion, Aristotle still considers them forms of change. We also saw that the substratum is spoken of both as being and as nonbeing. Although nothing comes to be without qualification from what is not, a thing may come to be from what is not in a qualified sense or by accident. According to *Physics* 1.9 (192a25–28), matter comes to be and ceases to be in one sense but not in another. As that which contains privation, it ceases to be because the privation is replaced by the corresponding form; but as the source of potentiality, it does not cease to be but is necessarily outside the sphere of coming to be and passing away.

Aristotle then goes on to make the following claim:[14]

> If it [matter] came to be, something must have existed as a primary substratum from which it should come and which should persist in it; but that is its own special nature so that it will be before coming to be. (For my definition of matter is just this – the primary substratum [*to prōton hupokeimenon*] of each thing, from which it comes to be without qualification, and which persists in the result.)

In a nutshell, matter cannot be generated because it is the principle that explains the generation of everything else. If one tried to explain how matter comes to be, he would find that he has no principle of explanation and therefore that the supposition on which he is working makes no sense. According to Maimonides' version of the argument, if prime matter were subject to generation, there would have to be a matter from which it is generated. In being generated, it would have to receive a form, for that is what generation means. Because by definition prime matter has no form, the

---

[14] Although generations of commentators have cited this passage as evidence that Aristotle believed in prime matter, W. Charlton (*Aristotle: Physics* 1–2, pp. 129–45) argues that this interpretation is due in large part to the tendency of people in late antiquity to force a synthesis between Plato and Aristotle.

notion that it takes on form in the process of being generated is absurd.

Once again the argument relies on the assumption that the generation of the world as a whole resembles the generation of individual things within it because both are natural processes that require a substratum. If we do not see plants or animals coming to be from nothing, why should we suppose the world does? Even if we did suppose it, how would we make sense of what we are saying? If the world were created *ex nihilo*, its coming to be would have no corollary in human experience. From a scientific perspective, this amounts to saying that it is a miracle – or worse, an absurdity.

The third argument has to do with the motion of the heavenly bodies and is found at *De Caelo* 1.3. We saw that coming to be is a transition from a substratum and privation to a substratum and the corresponding form. Passing away is the reverse. It follows that coming to be and passing away cannot occur unless we have contraries and a substratum to support them. Experience confirms that the heavenly bodies move in circular orbits for which there is no contrary, that is, no increase or decrease, no change of quality, no motion to or from the center of the earth. As Aristotle puts it (*De Caelo* 270b13–16): "In the whole range of time past, so far as our inherited records reach, no change appears to have taken place either in the whole scheme of the outermost heaven or in any of its proper parts." Needless to say, this argument suffers from the fact that although the planets generally appear to move from east to west, due to retrograde motion, there are times when they also appear to move from west to east.

Assuming that retrograde motion can be accounted for by adding additional spheres, the most reasonable conclusion is that the heavenly bodies are not *capable* of admitting contraries. If so, they are not capable of coming to be or passing away and therefore are eternal. Maimonides' version of this argument is a bit different.

He argues on the basis of similar reasoning that the heavenly bodies are not capable of passing away and then concludes that what cannot pass away cannot come to be.[15]

The fourth argument has to do with possibility. We saw from *On Generation and Corruption* 317b16–17 that coming to be implies the preexistence of something that potentially is but actually is not. This thing is the matter or substratum. If nothing can come to be without a substratum, something would have to exist prior to the creation of the world, from which it follows that creation is incoherent. As Davidson points out, this argument was reformulated by Avicenna, and it is that version that Maimonides repeats under the rubric of Aristotle's later followers.[16] Before the world came to be, its creation was possible, necessary, or impossible. If it was necessary, the world always had to exist and is eternal. If it was impossible, it would not exist now. If it was possible, it had to have a substratum that accounts for its possibility. If there is a substratum that preexists creation, creation is absurd.

It is worth noting, as Davidson does, that while all these arguments deal with the eternity of the world, they do not reach the same conclusion.[17] The second and fourth arguments establish the eternity of matter and would be accepted both by defenders of the Aristotelian position as described in *GP* 2.13 and by defenders of the Platonic. In effect these are arguments against creation *ex nihilo*. The third argument establishes the eternity of the cosmos and would be rejected by defenders of the Platonic position. The first argument establishes the eternity of motion and does not specify whether that motion involves the heavenly bodies; but given the way I have interpreted it, it belongs with the second and third.

---

[15] For the claim that what cannot pass away cannot have come to be, see *De Caelo* 282a22 ff.

[16] *PEC*, pp. 16–17.

[17] *PEC*, pp. 29–30.

II

Maimonides' overall response is to point out that these arguments are based on the same assumption: the origin of the world is analogous to the origin of a natural thing within it. Put otherwise, they assume that the principles one would use to explain the world as it is now can also explain its origin.[18] Recall that according to Maimonides (*GP* 2.13, p. 284), Aristotle is committed to the view that all that exists has been brought into existence *in the form in which it is at present.*

We saw that Aristotle does distinguish motion from coming to be and passing away. The problem is that coming to be and passing away are still explained in terms of act and potency. The thrust of Maimonides' criticism is that there is another step to take: the distinction between coming to be, which counts as a form of change, and creation, which does not. In whatever form we imagine it, change takes us from privation to fulfillment, both of which are ways of being and can be accounted for under the rubric of growth and reproduction. Creation, on the other hand, takes us from nonexistence to existence. It is the failure to consider creation as a possibility that mars Aristotle's arguments and leaves the impression that he has begged the question. This is part and parcel of the claim that Aristotle is concerned with the structure of the world, not its existence. The thrust of his arguments is that no matter how far back we go, that structure is inviolate.

Maimonides' reply is that the nature of a thing after it achieves stability may be different from the nature it has when it is generated, and that in turn may be different from the nature it has before it is generated.[19] This is true even in the case of observable phenomena for which we have an agent and a patient. Thus, the nature of the

---

[18] This strategy for replying to Aristotle is as old as Philoponus. See Simplicius' Commentary on Aristotle's *Physics* 1141, 5–30, as well as Philoponus, *Against Aristotle on the Eternity of the World* 114–16, pp. 128–30.

[19] For Gersonides' criticism of this argument, see Chapter 7.

feminine seed, which Maimonides identifies as the blood in the blood vessels, is different from its nature after it has encountered the male sperm. And both are different from a fully developed adult. Maimonides also remarks that in the generation of an animal, the heart comes to be before the testicles and the veins before the bones. After the animal is born, however, no part can exist unless all the essential parts exist together. Thus, any attempt to examine an adult and infer something about the way it came to be is fraught with peril. If this is true of observable phenomena, for which we can check ourselves at every stage of the process, why should we not think it is all the more true of the origin of the world, where we cannot?

To understand Maimonides' point, it would be helpful to recall his strategy: although both creation and eternity are subject to doubt, eternity is subject to greater doubt. This is because the proponents of eternity make a stronger claim. Their argument is not that eternity is preferable to creation but that creation is absurd. To support this argument, they have to trust a series of generalizations for which there is no evidence and no hope of finding any. How will we establish that the origin of the world bears any similarity to the growth of an animal from a seed? By contrast Maimonides is not claiming that eternity is absurd. All he is claiming is that knowledge of the world in its present state does not allow us to infer anything about its origin, so that, as far as we know, either view could be right. Maimonides even considers what to say if Aristotle or one of his followers should try to turn the tables. If we cannot prove eternity by inferring something from the world as it is now, how can you prove creation? The answer, of course, is that Maimonides is not trying to prove creation, only that creation is possible.

In making these arguments, Maimonides is not rejecting the science of his day. On the contrary, he is convinced it is right if we limit its application to the world after it has come into being and gained stability. From that standpoint, we cannot imagine motion coming to be or passing away as a whole. Nor can we imagine the generation or destruction of prime matter. The statement that circular motion has no contrary is correct; so, too, is the claim that possibility must precede actuality. But if we extend these principles beyond phenomena we can observe and apply them to the question of origin, we have nothing but conjecture.

If Maimonides' reply is successful, he has defended not only the possibility of creation *de novo* but that of creation *ex nihilo* as well. In fact, he says several times in *GP* 2.17 that he believes the world or its material component was brought into existence from nothing, from nonexistence, or from absolute nonexistence. Like the Greek *mē on*, the Arabic term *'adam* is ambiguous and can be used in an absolute sense, according to which it means nothing, or a relative one, according to which it means matter or privation. At *GP* 3.10, it has both senses, when Maimonides says that the Mutakallimūn do not imagine any nonbeing other than absolute nonbeing and thus do not recognize privations. I believe that in this context, there are reasons for taking in its absolute sense and ascribing creation *ex nihilo* to Maimonides.

First, he says in *GP* 2.13 that the Mosaic position is that God brought the world into existence "after having been purely and absolutely nonexistent."[20] As many people have noted, he uses several expressions to describe creation from nothing and often omits the qualification "pure and absolute."[21] The question is whether the

---

[20] Note that Maimonides often describes the Mosaic position as holding that God brought the world into existence *after* nothing (*ba'da al-'adam*) or *after* having been purely and absolutely nonexistent. I follow Wolfson (*SHPR*, Vol. 1, pp. 207–21) in arguing that in this context, *after* does not imply temporal passage. Grammatically "God created the world out of nothing" resembles "Susan made the statue out of bronze." So unless one is careful, "nothing" will appear to be the material cause of being. Because this is exactly what Maimonides wants to avoid, he speaks of creation after nothing rather than creation out of nothing. This corresponds to Aquinas' "post non esse."

[21] See Chapter 1, nn. 34 and 36. In addition to "after nothing" (*ba'd al-'adam*), Maimonides uses "out of nothing" (*min 'adam*), "not from a thing" (*lā min shay'*), or "from no thing" (*min lā shay'*). On the imperfection of language, note *GP* 1.57, pp. 133–32,

omission is significant or simply represents the fact that, like many philosophers of his day, Maimonides had not settled on a technical vocabulary in which a single idea is always designated by the same single term. Note that even in English, we often use "nothing," "nonbeing," and "nonexistence" as synonyms.

According to Sara Klein-Braslavy, Maimonides' failure to speak of pure and absolute nonbeing when characterizing his position at *GP* 2.30 and 3.10 indicates that he is not really committed to creation *ex nihilo*.[22] I suggest, however, that these passages can be read in a straightforward way. At *GP* 2.30 (pp. 348–49), Maimonides points out that although there are rabbinic precedents for the Platonic and Aristotelian views of creation, one should not be swayed by them because "I have already made it known to you that the foundation of the whole Law is the view that God brought the world into being out of nothing." This is a summary statement that refers back to Maimonides' original position, where the qualification "pure and absolute" was used. At *GP* 3.10, he reiterates his view that *bara* is connected with creation out of nothing. This refers back to the discussion at *GP* 2.30, where he rejects the Aristotelian and Platonic alternatives, both of which deny the possibility of creation *ex nihilo*. So although the phrase "pure and absolute" has been dropped, Maimonides gives the reader ample reason to think it is implied.

where Maimonides confesses that "the bounds of expression in all languages are very narrow indeed, so that we cannot represent this notion to ourselves except through a certain looseness of expression." Admittedly, he is talking about God in this passage, but given centuries of debate over the meaning of creation *ex nihilo*, it could easily apply to that subject as well. Again, see Wolfson, *SHPR*, Vol. 1, pp. 207–21

[22] Klein-Braslavy, 'The Creation," ibid. According to Klein-Braslavy (p. 69), Maimonides' arguments do not really lead to creation *ex nihilo*. That is because (1) he believes that neither creation nor eternity can be demonstrated and (2) the argument from particularity is not conclusive. The fact that neither position can be demonstrated does nothing to undermine the claim that Maimonides prefers creation. I will take up the argument from particularity in Chapter 6. Although not conclusive, given the scientific evidence available to Maimonides, it is still persuasive. Note furthermore that Maimonides defends creation *ex nihilo* at *GP* 2.17, where he distinguishes between generation and creation. The fact that prime matter is not subject to generation does not show that it is not created.

Aside from linguistic considerations, the arguments of *GP* 2.17 would make no sense if Maimonides took *nothing* to refer to matter or privation, for if that is what he meant, he would be espousing the very thing he set out to refute: the view that the origin of the world resembles the origin of a natural thing within it because both require a material cause. The problem is that as Maimonides presents the opinion of the philosophers (*GP* 2.13, 282–83), creation *ex nihilo* is not just hard to imagine but impossible to comprehend – like saying that God can create a square whose diagonal is equal to the side. It should be noted, however, that when Maimonides takes up the subject of logical possibility and impossibility at *GP* 3.15, he says clearly that "the bringing into being of a corporeal thing out of no matter whatever, belongs – according to us – to the class of the possible."

The claim that something cannot come from nothing (*ex nihilo nihil fit*) derives from Parmenides. Aristotle (*Physics* 191a31–191b17) agrees in the sense that nothing can come to be from what is not if we take "what is not" in its absolute or unqualified sense. His reason is that in coming to be, something must be present as a substratum. However plausible this may seem, it is part of a physical theory and hardly qualifies as a truth of logic. According to Maimonides, it is based on our experience of growth and reproduction, nothing more.

In one respect, Parmenides and the proponents of creation *ex nihilo* are in agreement, for the latter do not claim that it is a process by which nothing *becomes* something.[23] Here language can mislead us. Creation *out of* nothing does not commit one to the view that nothing is a material cause that is magically transformed into something. To avoid this kind of mistake, Maimonides and many of the medievals speak of creation *after* nothing.[24] Because there is

---

[23] This point was made by Philoponus. See Simplicius' commentary on *De Caelo* 136, 12–26; and Philoponus, *Against Aristotle on the Eternity of the World* 73, pp. 87–88.

[24] See n. 20.

no material cause, there is nothing that serves as the recipient of God's activity, nothing that is changed in the way that a substratum is changed when acted on by a agent. Rather creation *ex nihilo* affirms that everything owes its existence to God, so that without God, there would be nothing at all.[25] If this is true, creation *ex nihilo* amounts to the claim that everything, including matter, is generated. As Sorabji points out, and as I will try to show in the next chapter, the eternal generation of matter, which is to say its dependence on the first principle, is good Neoplatonism and was defended by a range of thinkers in this tradition.[26] Even Avicenna refers to eternal emanation as a creation *ba'da 'adam*.[27]

Why, then, does Maimonides say that none of the philosophers accept creation *ex nihilo?* The answer is that the philosophers do not accept it in the sense in which he understands it: that God created everything, including matter and form, *simultaneously*. There are two reasons for this. First, it supposes that a plurality can emerge from what is one and simple; second, that a material world can emerge from something that is pure form. The crux of the Neoplatonic position is that matter is not produced by God immediately but comes to be from a succession of intermediate causes. In Alfarabi and Avicenna, heavenly matter emerges when the first emanated intelligence thinks about itself as a being separate from God.[28] For Alfarabi, sublunar matter is produced by the power of the heavenly spheres; for Avicenna, by the movement of the heavenly spheres together with the activity of the agent intellect.[29]

We will see that Maimonides' view is very different. Even if we allow for a series of intermediate causes, there would still have to be a point where matter emerges from form. Because the introduction

---

[25] Cf. Aquinas, *On the Eternity of the World* 7 in *OTW*, p. 23, as well as Lenn Goodman, *God of Abraham*, p. 264.

[26] *TCC*, pp. 313–14.

[27] Avicenna, *Al-Shifā'* 266.

[28] Alfarabi, *Al-Madīna* 2.3.1–2, pp. 101–2; Avicenna, *Al-Shifā'* 406–7.

[29] *Al-Madīna* 3.8.1–5, pp. 135–43; *Al-Shifā'* 410–11.

of intermediate causes does not solve anything, it makes more sense to say that everything is created at once so that neither matter nor form presuppose something other than God. At bottom, God alone without any intermediaries is a sufficient cause of everything. That is his point of contention with the philosophers, not that matter exists independently of God.

It is well known that the *Gvide* is an esoteric work, so one cannot accept everything Maimonides says at face value. In this case, however, it is difficult to see what purpose esotericism would serve. If his reply to Aristotle contained a fallacy, one could argue that he expects the reader to spot it and conclude that Aristotle is right. I for one fail to see what the fallacy is. If the only grounds for rejecting the creation of everything *ex nihilo* are that we can find no analogue in nature and have difficulty imagining how it occurs, Maimonides is right to say that the philosophers have not succeeded in showing that it is impossible. He is also right that extrapolation from what we observe to the origin of the world is not trustworthy.

We will see in a later chapter that as his discussion of creation progresses, Maimonides becomes more critical of the science of his day. Not only does evidence from the world as it is now have no bearing on the question of its origin, there are current features of the world that science has not succeeded in explaining and, in Maimonides' opinion, never will. At that point Maimonides will try to make good on his claim that creation is preferable to eternity because it is subject to fewer doubts. At this juncture, all he wants to show is that it is possible.

### III

There remain arguments for eternity based on the nature of God. Here, too, Maimonides accuses the proponents of eternity of overreaching themselves. If, as Maimonides never tires of pointing out, the essence of God is beyond our comprehension, any argument that tries to determine what God can or cannot do based on knowledge of the divine essence is open to question. Maimonides agrees that God cannot do what is logically impossible. Thus, God cannot make a square whose diagonal is equal to its side.[30] But beyond logical absurdities, it is difficult for us to know what God is capable of. As we saw, the philosophers regard Maimonides' understanding of creation *ex nihilo* as impossible, but he thinks he has shown it is not.

In listing the arguments that proceed from the nature of God, Maimonides again makes clear that they are not necessarily the arguments of Aristotle himself but "those who came after him" (*GP* 2.14, p. 287). Unbeknown to Maimonides, most of these arguments derive from Proclus or the *Theology of Aristotle*.[31] In contrast to several of the arguments covered in the previous section, these deal with creation *de novo* rather than creation *ex nihilo*. In one way or another, they all follow a line of argument we encountered earlier in the *Theology*. The nature of the effect is determined by the nature of the cause; therefore, it is impossible for an eternal God to produce a temporal world. If the world came into existence at a particular point, God would have to be roused into activity to create it. But the arguments maintain: there is no way to explain God's being roused into activity in a coherent way.

The first argument says that if God created the world *de novo*, before creation God must have had the potential to create, while after creation that potential was actualized. What caused God to move from potency to act? Although Maimonides does not say anything further, the implication is that a believer in creation is faced

---

[30] See, for example, *GP* 3.15, pp. 459–61.

[31] For a Greek text and facing English translation of Proclus, see *On the Eternity of the World (De aeternitate mundi)*, ed. Helen S. Lang and A. D. Marco. The arguments contained in this volume are important not only for the eternity(creation debate but for the debate over which side Plato was on. As we saw, Proclus is a staunch proponent of the metaphorical reading of the *Timaeus*.

with a dilemma, either horn of which undercuts his case. If one replies that God does not go from potency to act but is always in act, God is not subject to change. If God is not subject to change, how can God be responsible for the creation of a world that is?

On the other hand, if one replies that something other than God is responsible for the transition from potency to act, we will ask what caused this thing to move from potency to act. If we keep going this way, an infinite regress will ensue. If whatever is responsible for God's transition from potency to act is always in act itself, God will always be in act, which again implies that creation of a temporal world is impossible. As Proclus says, an eternal, unchanging being must be active all the time or none of the time. If it always acts and acts in the same way, the effect it produces will always be the same as well.[32] Another way to see this point is to recognize that if God were in a potential state, the only way to account for that potency would be to attribute to God some kind of matter. Because it is agreed by all hands that God is immaterial, God must always be active.

The second argument is related to the first. If an agent acts at one time but not at another, the reason must be the presence of impediments or incentives. Impediments make it impossible for an agent to do what it wishes, and incentives make an agent wish for something it did not wish before. Because there are no impediments or incentives acting on God, no reason can be given for why God would act now but not later. As Aristotle asks (*De Caelo* 283a11–12): Why, after an infinity of not existing, would the world suddenly be generated at one moment rather than another?[33] Again the only reasonable conclusion is that God must always be active, from which it follows that the world must always exist.

---

[32] Proclus, *On the Eternity of the World*, pp. 140–141.

[33] Note Augustine's version of this argument at *City of God* 11.4: If God created the world at a particular point, God would be acting arbitrarily. As he shows in the next chapter, because there is no time prior to creation, it is misleading to picture God surveying an infinite number of indistinguishable times at which to create the world and picking one on whim.

The third argument is that God is perfect, and nothing God does contains a defect. If this is so, there cannot be any defects in what God has made or done. This conclusion is supported by Aristotle, who says that nature is perfect and does nothing in vain.[34] Clearly, then, the world is a product of divine wisdom. Because God's wisdom is eternal, the world must be eternal as well.

The fourth argument is a variation on the first and asks how God could be idle for an eternity before the world was created.[35] As Maimonides points out, it does not matter whether one thinks the world was created hundreds of thousands of years ago or yesterday, because in either case, the age of the world is finite, whereas God exists for eternity. The question is: what was God doing during the eternity before the world came to be? The only answer is nothing, which is obviously absurd.

To these arguments Maimonides adds another based on universal consent. Not surprisingly, he cites *De Caelo* 270b5–11, where Aristotle says that all people who believe in the existence of the gods, whether they are barbarian or Greek, "agree in allotting the highest place to the deity." In other words, the gods are immortal, the heavens are the dwelling place of the gods, therefore the heavens are immortal and not subject to generation or destruction.

IV

The strategy of these arguments is essentially the same: they assume the effect is a manifestation of the cause and therefore must resemble the cause. By the same token, if the cause is actual and present, the effect must follow and be simultaneous with it.[36] Any argument that shows the relation between cause and effect need

---

[34] *De Caelo* 271a33; *De Partibus Animalium* 695b18.
[35] Cf. Philo, *On Creation* 16.20, pp. 14–18.
[36] For an expression of this principle, see *Physics* 195b16–21.

not be as tight as the proponents of eternity think will count as an argument in defense of the possibility of creation *de novo*.

The obvious starting place is the will because the resemblance that obtains between a cause and its effect need not obtain between an act of will and the object willed in the act. There is no contradiction in saying that a single decision – the intention to write a book – can result in a wide array of activities spread over a long period of time. Nor is there a contradiction in saying that the will can be present and active while the object willed is postponed. According to what is commonly known as the principle of delayed effect, I can will now to raise my arm in five minutes or fifty-five minutes without interference from external factors. Simply put: the will does not have to bring about a given effect right away but can will what it wants when it wants.[37] From Maimonides' perspective, this means that it can particularize its object, which is another way of saying that it can choose its object and the time of its appearance from a range of alternatives.

Maimonides' reply to the arguments from the nature of God owe much to the Kalām. It is well known that he is often critical of the Mutakallimūn, saying that they do not distinguish between genuine argument and flights of fancy. In considering his relation to these thinkers, we should keep several points in mind. First, he does not accept atomism. Second, although he thinks that an appeal to divine volition is a legitimate form of explanation in some cases, he does not think, as many of the Mutakallimūn did, that it is the only legitimate form or that divine volition is arbitrary and exhibits the liberty of indifference.[38] Third, he does not think creation can be demonstrated. So there is much that separates Maimonides and

---

[37] Cf. Aquinas, *Summa Contra Gentiles* (*OTW*), p. 35: "Just as the will determines that a thing should be of a definite nature, so it wills that the thing should exist at a particular time."

[38] On this issue, see *GP* 1.73, p. 202: "They assert that when a man moves a pen, it is not the man who moves it; for the motion occurring in the pen is an accident created by God in the pen."

the Mutakallimūn, even though they are in agreement that the arguments for eternity are not valid.

The crux of Maimonides' reply to these arguments is that they are valid only for a being that is a composite of matter and form. When such a being acts after a period of not acting, there is a transition from potency to act. But this is not the case for a being that is neither a body nor a force within a body. In Maimonides' words (*GP* 2.18, p. 299): "The acts of forms endowed with matter and the acts of a separate being are both called 'act' only by equivocation."

Recall that the first argument asks what is responsible for God's transition from potency to act. The reply is nothing because God is always in act. If it is asked how a being that is always in act can do something at one time and not at another, Maimonides replies that there is a precedent for this in Alfarabi's treatise "On the Intellect."[39] There Alfarabi claims that if the agent intellect acts at some times and not at others, the reason is not that its essence has changed but that the matter on which it acts has not been prepared to receive the action, that an impediment from outside has interfered with the matter, or both. So when we say the agent intellect acts now and not then, we are speaking of its effects. As Maimonides recognizes, this example is problematic because it assumes eternity. What he takes from it is that even in the Aristotelian tradition, intermittent action does not necessarily imply change in the agent. So there is no reason to think that change in the agent is the only possible explanation. When he gets to volition, Maimonides introduces an alternative.

The second argument had to do with impediments and incentives. It is true, Maimonides admits, that for an agent who strives to realize an external end such as building a house, that intermittent action can be explained by the presence of impediments and

[39] For an English translation, see *Philosophy in the Middle Ages*, 2d ed., ed. Arthur Hyman and James J. Walsh, pp. 215–21.

incentives such as cost, weather, and availability of materials. This is not true, however, of an agent that has no need of external ends and acts in a purely autonomous fashion. To the question "What motivated God to act now and not then?" the answer is that God is self-motivated.

The obvious objection to Maimonides is that willing something now and something else later does constitute a change. Maimonides replies that this is not true, because the ability to will or not will is what it means to have a will in the first place. Thus "the fact that it may wish one thing now and a different thing tomorrow does not constitute a change in its essence and does not call for another cause" (*GP* 2.18, p. 301). There is little doubt that Maimonides is appealing to a distinction that originated in Augustine and found expression in Philoponus and Alghazali.[40] I can will today something that will not be accomplished until tomorrow and something completely different the next day without interference from outside factors. It does not follow that each time I undertake a different action, there must be a different act of will behind it. The usual way of making this point is to distinguish between willing change and changing one's will. The crux of the distinction is that to will change is not necessarily to undergo change; rather, it is to carry on with what one always intended. As applied to God, this means that a perfect being can will that a temporal world come into existence at a particular point, develop a nature appropriate to it, and keep to that nature for the rest of time.

Behind the distinction between willing change and changing one's will is the recognition that the will is not a natural phenomenon that needs a cause to stir it into activity. As Augustine says elsewhere, an act of will has no cause unless one wants to say

---

[40] Augustine, *City of God* 11.4, 12.15 and 18; Philoponus, *On The Eternity of the World* (ed. Rabe), pp. 78, 568, 613; Alghazali, *The Incoherence of the Philosophers*, pp. 15–17. Also see Aquinas *ST* 1.46.1.

that it is the cause of itself.[41] This means that there is no need for something to take the will from potency to act; it is always in act or always spontaneous. By the same token, there are no grounds for asserting a resemblance between an act of will and the object willed in the act. We have already seen that it is possible to will change endlessly or to will a complicated course of action in a split second. So even though the will is active and a sufficient cause for initiating a certain action, the act may not occur for a long time, and in some cases, may never occur. If it is asked why it does not occur, the only valid reply is that the agent willed not to do it.

Although Maimonides is not this explicit, he does see that the categories of cause and change do not apply to the will. One of the virtues of introducing volition is that it frees us from the need to ask what he regards as silly – even disgraceful – questions about God's motivation. If there is an explanation for everything God does, people will ask why God created the world at one moment rather than another, why God gave the Law to a particular person at a particular time, or why God required the sacrifice of a lamb in one instance and the sacrifice of a ram in another.[42] Maimonides' answer is this (*GP* 2.25, p. 329):

> He wanted it this way; or His wisdom required it this way. And just as He brought the world into existence, having the form it has, when He wanted to, without our knowing His will with regard to this or in what respect there was wisdom in His particularizing the forms of the world and the time of its creation – in the same way we do not know His will or the exigency of His wisdom that caused all the matters, about which questions have been posed above, to be particularized.

Like Augustine, Maimonides rejects the suggestion that God surveyed an infinite number of alternatives when deciding to create

---

[41] Augustine, *On Free Will* 202, p. 83.
[42] The reference to sacrifices comes from *GP* 3.26, p. 509.

the world and chose one arbitrarily.[43] The point is rather that if God is going to create the world *de novo*, at any point in its history, the world must have a specific age. It is true that one can always ask why it is this age rather than that, but in Maimonides' opinion, nothing follows from this except the obvious point that the search for reasons cannot go on indefinitely.

It is important that we understand what Maimonides is trying to say. He does not believe, in fact he repeatedly denies, that God acts on whim or caprice.[44] In addition to people who seek a motive for everything, there are those who seek it for nothing and refer all phenomena, from the age of the world to the design of specific things within it, to the will of God. According to them, all the possibilities that God surveys are equally valid so that the choice of one over another is completely arbitrary. It is well known that the Mutakallimūn carry this reasoning to its extreme. In Maimonides' judgment (*GP* 1.74, p. 218):

> Thus they say: the earth's being under the water is not more appropriate than its being above the water. Who then has particularized that place for it? And the sun's being circular is not more appropriate than its being square or triangular, as all shapes bear the same relation to the bodies endowed with shapes. Who therefore has particularized the sun in respect of the shape it has? They consider in a similar way all the particulars of the world as a whole.

In short the Mutakallimūn do not see any natural reason why God made the world one way rather than another and refer anything that is conceivable otherwise to God's ability to pick between equal alternatives.

---

[43] To the question "Why did God not create the world a moment sooner?" Augustine answers (*City of God* 11.5–6) that because there was no time before creation, the question makes no sense. Cf. Philoponus, *On the Eternity of the World* (ed. Rabe), pp. 11–12.

[44] See, for example, *GP* 3.25, 3.26.

Maimonides objects that if this view is right, God's actions would be futile or frivolous because they would not accomplish anything, making it impossible to ascribe wisdom to God.[45] To return to the issue of sacrifice, we may not be able to know why a lamb is required in this instance and a ram in that; but given the historical climate in which these laws were promulgated, Maimonides thinks they served "a great and manifest utility."[46] From the fact that our understanding of this utility does include every detail, it does not follow that God decided the matter by flipping a coin. All that follows is that the specifics of sacrifice are contingent matters for which no satisfactory explanation is available. The same holds for the age of the world. The fact that we cannot discern a reason for its age does not imply that the world is eternal or that God acted whimsically in creating it.

Like the other proofs, the third is based on the resemblance between cause and effect. If the world is a manifestation of God's wisdom, and that wisdom is eternal and unchanging, we seem to be faced with the conclusion that the world is unchanging as well.[47] The problem is the ease with which the premises are offered. If we are ignorant of the true nature of God's wisdom and our knowledge of how the world proceeds from that wisdom is speculative, we are in no position to infer anything about the age of the world. Thus, Maimonides' reply (*GP* 2.19, p. 302): "The world is consequent upon His perpetual and immutable wisdom. But we are completely ignorant of the rule of that wisdom and of the decision made by it." Just as we do not know what wisdom there is in having nine spheres, or a certain number of stars, we do not know the wisdom in having the world be one age rather than another. We can agree

---

[45] *GP* 3.25, p. 504.

[46] *GP* 3.26, p. 509. For his explanation of that utility, see 3.32, pp. 525–27.

[47] Note how this argument survives in Spinoza, *Ethics* 1.29: "Nothing in nature is contingent, but all things are from the necessity of the divine nature determined to exist and to act in a definite way."

that whatever the reasons may be, God's wisdom is perfect. But it does not follow from this that we can infer something specific about the age or eternity of the world.

Defenders of contingency always face the question of whether their claim is epistemological or ontological – that *we* cannot find a reason why something is the way it is or that at bottom there is no reason. That Maimonides is committed to contingency as an epistemological claim is clear from his responses to Aristotle. The question is whether his commitment runs deeper. From the passages we have examined, the implication is that unbeknown to us, God did have a reason for picking a certain age for the world, a certain number of stars, or possibly one form of sacrifice over another. In fact, this seems to be what Maimonides asserts (*GP* 3.25, p. 505):

> For while we believe that the world was produced in time, none of our scholars and none of our men of knowledge believe that this came about through the will and nothing else. For they say that His wisdom ... the apprehension of which is beyond us – obligatorily necessitated the existence of this world as a whole at the moment when it came into existence, and that the selfsame immutable wisdom necessitated nonexistence before the world came into existence.... Such is the belief of the multitude of the men of knowledge in our Law, and this was explicitly stated by our prophets: namely, that the particulars of natural acts are all well arranged and ordered and bound up with one another, all of them being causes and effects; and that none of them is futile or frivolous or vain, being acts of perfect wisdom.

Unfortunately, this passage and the one from 2.25 quoted earlier are obviously equivocal. Is the world the product of divine will, divine wisdom, or both?

On the surface, Maimonides is not always consistent on the relation between will and wisdom. When he wants to distance himself from Aristotle and argue that there are facts for which we have no explanation, he talks as if the world is the product of will.[48] When he wants to distance himself from the Mutakallimūn and defend causal explanation, he talks, as he does at *GP* 3.25, as if it is the product of wisdom.[49] At *GP* 2.18 (p. 302), he claims that will is consequent on wisdom. In several places, he talks as if the distinction between them is unimportant, so that one can look at the world as the product of either one.[50] A good example of the latter is *GP* 3.14 (p. 456), where he says that when we give up the need to seek reasons for everything, our soul becomes calm because we accept the fact that some things depend for their existence on the divine will, or "if you prefer you can also say: on the divine wisdom."

It would be wrong to read these passages as evidence of relaxed standards of rigor. The suggestion that one can look at the world as the product of will *or* wisdom derives from the fact that will and wisdom cannot be separate faculties in God as they are in us. Although he sometimes implies that will is consequent on wisdom, Maimonides also implies that wisdom has the power to choose between alternatives.[51] In view of his commitment to negative theology, we should not take these passages as an invitation to engage in speculation on the inner workings of God or how it is that God brings about one result rather than another. The thrust of his remarks is rather to direct attention away from God to the world.

Our knowledge of the world is based on observation. In cases for which science can furnish adequate explanations of what we observe or jurisprudence can furnish adequate explanations of what we are obliged to do, it is foolish to invoke the will of God or, as Maimonides puts it, to invoke will and nothing else. But it does not

---

[48] See for example, *GP* 2.21, p. 316, and 3.13, pp. 452–54.

[49] Also see *GP* 3.26, p. 506.

[50] *GP* 1.69, p. 170; 2.25, p. 329; 2.27, pp. 332–33. Cf. Aquinas, *ST* 1.19.4.

[51] See *GP* 2.19, p. 302; 3.25, pp. 505–6; 3.26, p. 509.

follow that we are justified in seeking explanations for everything. When science or jurisprudence cannot furnish explanations, we have no choice but to say that God wanted it that way and give up the need to find out why. Because we assume God does not act on whim or caprice, we must suppose there are reasons for choosing one alternative over another even if we cannot discern what they are. According to *GP* 3.49 (p. 605): "Our intellects are incapable of apprehending the perfection of everything that He has made and the justice of everything He has commanded."

Still, the existence of reasons does not necessarily rule out contingency. The question is whether the reasons God has for doing something are such that no alternative is possible or whether alternatives are possible but from God's perspective not desirable. In the next chapter, I argue that Maimonides' use of the argument from particularity shows that there are features of the world for which alternatives clearly exist. For the present, we can simply say that the connection between will and wisdom in God is supposed to rule out both arbitrariness and strict adherence to necessity. As Leibniz would say centuries later, God has reasons that incline without necessitating.[52]

Maimonides has not shown, nor has he claimed to show, that God actually possesses free will. What he has shown is (1) nothing prevents us from thinking so and (2) unless we accept free will in God, we will be in the embarrassing position of having to deny contingency altogether. By contrast, if God has free will, there is no reason why God had to create the world, because he could have willed or not willed to do so. In a later chapter, we will see that contingency is not only compatible with purpose but required. As Maimonides puts it (*GP* 2.21, p. 314): "The notions of purpose and particularization only apply to a nonexistent thing for which it is

---

[52] Leibniz, *The Leibniz-Clarke Correspondence* (Alexander), p. 56. Also see *Discourse on Metaphysics* (Lucas and Grint), pp. 19–22.

possible to exist just as it was purposed and particularized and for which it also is possible not to exist in this fashion."[53]

It is important to recognize that when Maimonides talks about purpose, he means more than simple performance of a function. If Aristotle is right, and the world exists by necessity, there could still be things that serve a purpose in the sense that they contribute to the well-being of something else. What there would not be is any alternative to these things. Recall that for Aristotle eternity implies necessity: if the order we find in nature always was and always will be, no other order is possible.

Not surprisingly, Maimonides claims (*GP* 2.22, p. 319) that if Aristotle is right, even trivial things such as the shape of a fly's wing or the length of a worm's foot could not be otherwise. Although both may be needed for the animal to survive, Maimonides' point is that this is not enough. Even if a particular organ is needed for an animal to survive, there is still the question of what purpose the animal's existence serves. If it has to exist, it is pointless to ask what purpose an agent had in bringing it to be. That is why Maimonides argues that we can have purpose only if the thing in question has not always existed, which is to say only if its existence is not necessitated.

Because God's existence is necessary, it makes no sense to ask what purpose it serves. Such is not the case when it comes to God's act of conferring existence on other things. If Maimonides is right, God could have created a different world or no world at all. As long as this is true, contingency is not just a limitation of human knowledge but a fundamental feature of the world we inhabit. In his words (*GP* 3.13, p. 452): "What exists, its causes, and its effects, could be different from what they are." That sentiment underlies his conviction that for everything for which existence is due to an external cause, existence is an accident. I take this to mean not

---

[53] Cf. *GP* 2.19, p. 303.

only that existence is not a part of essence but that nothing in the nature of God or the nature of the world requires that the essence in question be realized: in short, existence attaches to essence as a result of a free choice.

Although there is no formal reply to the idleness argument, it is not difficult to imagine Maimonides saying, with Augustine, that because there is no time before creation, the claim that God is idle during that period amounts to nonsense. Finally there is the universal agreement that the gods are important and dwell in heaven. Maimonides points out that something similar can be found in the sacred literature of Judaism if we are talking about the angels or separate intellects. But in Judaism this does not count as a proof that the heavens are eternal; it is rather a proof that there are spiritual beings. Because I take up Maimonides' view of the heavens in the next chapter, I skip over this material for now.

V

Putting together both of Maimonides' sets of replies, we can see the full extent of his disagreement with Aristotle. The problem with arguments from the nature of the world is that creation is not subject to observation; the problem with arguments from the nature of God is that divine wisdom is beyond our comprehension. In each case, Aristotle uses principles derived from natural philosophy to shed light on theology. The reason is clear. As Norbert Samuelson points out, for someone who is neither a prophet nor heir to a prophetic tradition, the only place to start is with premises derived from experience.[54] If the application of these premises is valid, creation in any form is absurd. Maimonides' reply is that for those who are heir to a prophetic tradition, the application of natural philosophy to theology begs an important question. Why

---

54 Samuelson, "Maimonides' Doctrine," p. 255.

should we assume that principles that apply to the sublunar realm also apply to the heavens? Recall that for him, even the claim that God's wisdom is greater than ours presupposes too much because it describes God in terms borrowed from human experience. By applying the categories of act and potency to God, we make the same mistake.

This raises the question of whether Aristotle thought his arguments for eternity constituted a demonstration. Although he admits that most of Aristotle's followers think the answer is yes, Maimonides tries to argue (*GP* 2.15) that the answer is really no. In this connection, he cites three passages. The first is *Physics* 251b15, where Aristotle says that Plato alone believed that motion is subject to generation and corruption. Why, asks Maimonides, would Aristotle appeal to common consent if he thought his position could be demonstrated? The second is *De Caelo* 279b4 ff., where Aristotle says that he will cite the opinions of those who disagree with him so that no one can accuse him of trying to secure victory by default. The last is *Topics* 104b13–17, where Aristotle claims that the eternity of the world is so vast a question that it is difficult to give reasons for it.

Maimonides' reading of these passages is far from cogent because Aristotle does give detailed arguments on behalf of eternity. As is often the case, Aristotle buttresses these arguments with appeals to observation, common sense, the opinions of other philosophers, and anything else he thinks will strengthen his case. The reason his followers thought he did have a demonstration of eternity is that eternity is a crucial premise of his proof for the existence of God. If that premise is not susceptible to demonstration, the whole proof would be thrown into doubt: if the world were only finitely many years old, it would be possible for a finite body to keep itself in motion for the entire history of the world, making it unnecessary to posit an incorporeal first mover.

From Maimonides' perspective, the arguments for eternity cannot be demonstrations because they presuppose knowledge no one can have. When he says at *GP* 2.25 that he would interpret the opening lines of Genesis in accord with eternity if it could be demonstrated, he is not conceding much. It is important to understand that the context in which Maimonides is working is different from that afforded by modern astrophysics because the only theories of creation he considers are those that affirm the existence of God. To demonstrate creation and not just extrapolate from knowledge already at hand one, would have to acquire certainty on what God is and how divine actions proceed from the divine essence. If Maimonides' negative theology teaches us anything, it is that this goal cannot be attained. Thus: "The Law has given us knowledge of a matter the grasp of which is not in our power" (*GP* 2.25, p. 329). This accords with what he says earlier at *GP* 2.17 (p. 294), when he claims that creation *de novo* should be accepted "without proof because of prophecy, which explains things to which it is not in the power of speculation to accede."

Here, then, is a case where skeptical doubts favor the prophetic tradition rather than the philosophic. When Maimonides says that prophecy should be accepted without proof, he does not mean that it should be accepted uncritically. Rather, he means that one should not wait for a proof of creation to make up one's mind, because a convincing proof is not within our power. This makes sense only if the arguments against creation have been answered and its possibility defended.

Unfortunately, Maimonides' appeal to the prophetic tradition causes problems of its own. We saw that the opening lines of Genesis are obscure and that there was considerable disagreement on how to interpret them. In the passage from *GP* 2.25 just cited, Maimonides says that one could interpret this and similar texts in accordance with the Platonic position:

> However, no necessity could impel us to do this unless this opinion [Plato's] were demonstrated. In view of the fact that it has

not been demonstrated, we shall not favor this opinion, nor shall we heed that other opinion [Aristotle's], but rather shall take the texts according to their external sense.

The reference to the external sense of the texts refers to the position of Moses, which affirms a creation that is both *ex nihilo* without the existence of intermediate causes and *de novo*. The problem with this passage is that it appears to conflict with *GP* 2.17 (p. 298), where Maimonides says that Scripture must *not* be taken in its external sense, as he will later show at greater length.

I follow Pines in taking Maimonides' reference to a later discussion to mean *GP* 2.30, where he goes into detail on the first six days of creation. We saw that in that chapter, there are many warnings against taking words in their external sense, among them *earth, fire, darkness*, and, most important, *water*. He also warns against taking references to days in their external sense, arguing that everything was created simultaneously and that things then gradually became differentiated. It is worth remarking that when he sides with Aristotle, he does so without hesitation.[55] There are no secrets to unravel or smoke screens to get through. That is because he thinks Aristotle has a cogent account of how meteorological phenomena work. When established facts contradict the external sense of the text, the external sense must be abandoned.

No such account forces him to abandon his interpretation of the opening line of Genesis. In fact, he repeats the traditional view in the same chapter (*GP* 2.30, p. 349), saying that the foundation of the Law is the belief that God created the world *ex nihilo* "without there having been a temporal beginning. For time is created, being consequent upon the motion of the sphere, which is created." Again I take the rejection of temporal creation to be a rejection of the view that the world was created *in* time and an assertion that it was created together *with* time. If Maimonides wanted to agree with

[55] *GP* 2.30, p. 353.

Aristotle about the opening line of Genesis, nothing would have prevented him from saying so, because Jewish thinkers sided with Aristotle before Maimonides and continued to do so after him. The fact is that he does not side with Aristotle on this point and offers powerful reasons why.

# 4

# Plotinus and Metaphysical Causation

WHATEVER THEIR DIFFERENCES, THE DEMIURGE IN Plato's *Timaeus* and the Prime Mover in Aristotle's *Metaphysics* have this much in common: both are finite beings whose purpose is to explain a feature of the world, not everything about it. The Demiurge imposes order on a preexistent chaos that he has not created and over which he has only limited control. The Prime Mover is the last in a series of causes needed to explain the eternal motion of the heavens but does nothing to explain why they are there in the first place.

It is clear that this picture of the world is subject to a serious objection: How can we understand something whose existence is ungenerated? After all, *ungenerated* is another name for *unexplained*. Plotinus' great achievement is that he gives us a higher level of abstraction. No longer is the question how to explain this or that feature but how to explain the world as a whole. According to what may be his best-known insight, it is impossible to understand anything unless we view it as *one* of something.[1] Thus, everything that is, insofar as it is, owes its existence to the first principle, or as Plotinus calls it, the One. The first principle is the common source (*archē*) of all things because everything is derived from it and nothing can exist without it. Insofar as it is the source of existence, it is also the source of value. According to *EN* 5.5.9, it is the good of everything "because all things have their being directed towards it and depend on it, each in a different way."

Gone is the idea that one principle is needed to explain form, another to explain matter, or that they are locked in some sort of conflict.[2] Instead, all of reality is an outgrowth of an infinite and transcendent power unlike anything available to the senses. Needless to say, this idea played a critical role in the development of monotheism and greatly influenced Maimonides. Although both Plato and Aristotle took certain features of existence as given, that is not how Maimonides reads them. He assumes they, too, believed that everything proceeds from a single source. The question is whether that source exercises free will or is governed by necessity.

Despite the differences between Plotinus' first principle and Plato's Demiurge, the influence of the latter on the former is unmistakable in light of *Republic* 509b, where Plato says that goodness is superior to and beyond being in dignity and power. For both thinkers, superiority is not just a way of ranking things but a way of establishing ontological dependence. In the comparison between goodness and the sun, Plato says (ibid.): "The sun not only gives to the objects of sight the capacity to be seen, but also provides for their generation, increase, and nurture." At 517c, he goes on to say

---

[1] *EN* 6.9.1, 6.9.2. Cf. Gilson, *Being and Some Philosophers*, p. 11: "That which is, is bound to be one, because it is contradictory to conceive as belonging to a certain being something *other than* that being."

[2] I will have more to say later about the generation of matter.

that goodness is the cause (*aitia*) of all that is right and beautiful and that in the intelligible world it both produces and controls truth and intelligence. But the precise meaning of this passage is unclear. How is goodness a cause? Is it also a cause of sensible things? Does it affect them even if they are not right and beautiful?

Beyond these questions, there is the general question of how to characterize something that is prior to everything else. Although Plato says a fair amount *about* goodness in establishing its unique position in the intelligible world, he says comparatively little when it comes to what it is. It is not a species of a genus or the effect of a prior cause. It is not definable in terms of other things because it is prior to them. It has no parts into which it can be broken or greater wholes into which it can be subsumed. For all intents and purposes, the only thing one can do is eliminate false pretenders to the crown and hope that the true nature of goodness becomes apparent.

In Plotinus the dependence of all things on a single source is not a conjecture but a fundamental doctrine. Still, we must be careful not to read biblical doctrines into a thinker who is still under the sway of ancient Greece. As we saw in our discussion of the *Timaeus, generation* for Plotinus does not refer to creation *de novo* but to eternal dependence. According to *EN* 2.9.3: "Things that are said to have come into being did not just come into being [at a particular moment] but always were and always will be in process of becoming."[3] And 3.2.1: "We affirm that this universe is everlasting and has never not existed." In short, the primary issue for Plotinus is still one of structure.

As one might expect, a higher level of abstraction brings with it a new set of problems. The imposition of form on matter is a simple process that can be observed and repeated. The reliance of all things on an infinite and transcendent source is not. For present

---

[3] The material in brackets is added by Armstrong. Also see *EN* 2.4.5, 5.1.6.

purposes, Plotinus is important because he raises what became the central question for Maimonides if not for medieval philosophy in general. In the words of *EN* 5.1.6, the soul longs to know how from the first principle, which is simple and lacks nothing, anything else came to be. Why, for example, did the first principle not remain by itself? And, if it did not, how did it cause other things? How, that is, can many come to be from one?

I

The crux of Plotinus' view is expressed at *EN* 5.4.1:

> There must be something simple before all things, and this must
> be other than all the things which come after it, existing by itself,
> not mixed with the things which derive from it, and all the same
> able to be present in a different way to these other things, being
> really one, and not a different being and then one; it is false even
> to say of it that it is one, and there is "no concept or knowledge"
> of it; it is indeed also said to be "beyond being."

The first principle must be simple and unmixed because if it were complex, it would be the effect of prior causes and no longer a first principle. Because all things come from it, nothing can limit it or influence it. It does not have relations to anything else because it is simple and completely self-sufficient.[4] In Plotinus' words, it seeks nothing, has nothing, and needs nothing.[5]

But there is more to *EN* 5.4.1 than an affirmation of simplicity – there is the additional claim that the first principle must be "other than the things which come after it." This doctrine is expressed more fully at *EN* 5.5.6:

> Since the substance which is generated [from the One] is
> form . . . and not the form of some one thing but of everything,

[4] *EN* 6.8.8.
[5] *EN* 5.2.1.

99

so that no other form is left outside it, the One must be without form. But if it is without form it is not a substance; for a substance must be some one particular thing, something, that is, defined and limited; but it is impossible to apprehend the One as a particular thing: for then it would not be the principle, but only that particular thing which you said it was. But if all things are in that which is generated [from the One], which of the things in it are you going to say the One is? Since it is none of them, it can only be said to be beyond them. But these things are beings, and being: so it is "beyond being."

By its very nature, form implies limitation: it makes something this rather than that. As the source of all being, the first principle is beyond being and thus form *less*. Although Plotinus calls it the One or the Good and at various times endows it with existence, life, power, actuality, or self-sufficiency, these descriptions should not be understood as attributes in the normal sense of the term but as ways of directing the mind to an ineffable reality.[6] Thus the passage continues: "We in our travail do not know what we ought to say, and are speaking of what cannot be spoken, and give it a name because we want to indicate it to ourselves as best we can."[7]

From a historical perspective, Plotinus' first principle fills the gap left by Aristotle's Prime Mover insofar as it is not only the goal toward which existence strives but the source from which it proceeds, the final and the efficient cause together.[8] Even so, we must be careful not to foist on Plotinus an Aristotelian understanding of efficient causality. For the latter, efficient causality is typically a horizontal relation in which one substance imparts motion to another as when a builder builds a house. For Plotinus, this is not

---

[6] *EN* 5.3.13.

[7] Cf. *GP* 1.57, p. 133: "For this reason, we give the gist of the notion and give the mind the correct direction toward the true reality of the matter when we say one but not through oneness"; and 1.58, p. 135: "They [negative attributes] conduct the mind toward the utmost reach that man may attain in the apprehension of Him."

[8] *EN* 6.8.14. For further expressions of efficient causality, see *EN* 3.8.10, 5.2.1, 5.3.15, 5.5.5, 6.8.14.

true. As we will see, the causality manifested by the first principle is not a consequence of what it does but simply of what it is.[9] Its effects flow from it in a manner that is continuous, necessary, and unintentional. So although the first principle is responsible for the existence of the world, this is not due to any movement it makes or inclination it feels.

More important, Plotinus does not think of causality as a horizontal relation. Because it derives its existence from the cause, the effect is not another thing standing alongside the cause but an imperfect manifestation – what Plotinus, in keeping with his Platonic heritage, calls an image or trace. In this way, Plotinian causality involves a falling away from the cause, so that what generates is always superior to what is generated.[10] Triangularity is superior to a physical triangle because it is the essence without any of the deficiencies or imperfections that come with physical things. One way to understand superiority is in terms of simplicity. The essence exists by itself without size, color, or spatial location; the thing that embodies the essence also embodies other qualities and no longer exists by itself.

Finally, Plotinian causality is not temporal. Although it makes sense to ask whether a builder is proceeding quickly or slowly, it makes no sense to ask this when dealing with the relation between an essence and the thing that embodies it. For a Platonist, there cannot be *a* triangle unless there is triangularity. But the latter takes no action to construct triangles or prevent them from being destroyed; it simply tells us what it is to be a triangle in the first place.

The precedent for Plotinus' view can be found at *Phaedo* 99d–101b, where Socrates says that what makes something beautiful is

---

9 On this point, see Cristina D'Ancona Costa, "Plotinus and Later Platonic Philosophers on the Causality of the First Principle," *CCP*, pp. 356–68. Cf. A. H. Armstrong, *Plotinus: A Volume of Selections*, p. 33: "*Nous* proceeds from the One (and soul from *Nous*) without in any way affecting its Source. There is no activity on the part of the One, still less any willing or planning or choice."

10 *EN* 3.8.9.

not a particular color or shape but the presence of, or participation in, beauty itself. The idea is that if we explain beauty by referring to a particular color, we will find that in another context we explain ugliness by referring to the same thing. If so, the explanation of what makes something beautiful must go deeper. Why are color, shape, or anything else contributing factors to beauty? What do these things share that makes them worthy of being called *beautiful*? Plato uses the word *aitia* and the causal dative to express the fact that beauty is responsible for all beautiful things. He obviously does not mean that beauty produces instances of itself in the way that a sculptor produces a statue but that there would be no instances of beauty unless there were something in which they participate.

Still, participation is not the same as efficient causality. To say that all beautiful things share a certain feature is not to say why there are beautiful things. Following *Timaeus* 29e, where Plato suggests that perfection manifests itself as abundance, Plotinus claims it is a universal feature of reality that things try to produce copies or offspring according to their degree of perfection. Thus *EN* 5.1.6:

> All things which exist, as long as they remain in being, necessarily produce from their own substances [*ousias*], in dependence on their present power, a surrounding reality directed to what is outside them, a kind of image of the archetypes from which it was produced: fire produces the heat which comes from it, snow does not only keep its cold inside itself. Perfumed things show this particularly clearly. As long as they exist, something is diffused from themselves around them, and what is near them enjoys their existence. And all things when they come to perfection produce [*genna*]; the One is always perfect and therefore produces everlastingly.

Note the generality of the passage. All things, from those that do not exercise choice to those that do, contribute a measure of their perfection to what is outside them.[11] If fire, snow, and perfume

---

[11] Also see *EN* 5.4.1.

generate traces or copies of themselves, according to Plotinus, it is impossible for the most perfect thing of all not to generate anything.[12]

In the next treatise (5.4.2), he formulates the doctrine with greater precision:

> In each and every thing there is an activity which belongs to substance [*energeia tēs ousias*] and one which goes out from substance [*energeia ek tēs ousias*]; and that which belongs to substance is the active actuality which is each particular thing, and the other activity derives from that first one, and must in everything be a consequence of it, different from the thing itself: as in fire there is a heat which is the content of its substance, and another which comes into being from that primary heat when fire exercises the activity which is native to its substance in abiding unchanged as fire. So it is also in the higher world; and much more so there, while the Principle abides "in its own proper way of life," the activity generated from the perfection of it and its coexistent activity acquires substantial existence, since it comes from a great power, the greatest indeed of all, and arrives at being and substance.

Although the reference to *energeia* calls to mind Aristotle, as Lloyd Gerson notes, Plotinus adds a new twist.[13] For Aristotle, activity is usually self-contained. The act of seeing is complete in itself, and there is no suggestion that it must issue in or contribute to

---

[12] *EN* 5.4.1.

[13] Lloyd P. Gerson, "Plotinus' Metaphysics: Emanation or Creation?" *Review of Metaphysics* 46 (1993): 566–70. Although this article contains much that is valuable, I take issue with the general strategy of trying to minimize the difference between Plotinus and an avowed creationist like Aquinas. It is true that Plotinus says that the first principle acts according to its will at 6.8.13, but as I indicate later, this comment comes with serious qualifications. What Gerson must show is that *will* as it is used in Plotinus has the same general meaning as it has for Aquinas. Note, however, that for the latter (*ST* 1.19.3), it is not necessary for God to will anything but himself. Therefore, although God knows necessarily everything he knows, it is not true that he wills necessarily everything he wills. In particular, it is not necessary for God to will the existence of the world (1.46.1), so if he wills it, it is not by necessity. It is possible then that the world might not exist. I see nothing like this even on Rist's reading of *EN* 6.8.13.

something external.[14] The same is true of thought. The Prime Mover thinks eternally. Although other things may emulate his thought, he is not responsible for generating anything in Plotinus' sense of the term. For a Platonist it is otherwise. As described in *Republic* 517, the sun is both active in itself and the source from which the activity of light radiates.

Although comparisons with fire, snow, and sunlight are helpful to a point, Plotinus recognizes that they are problematic.[15] Sunlight emanates from a particular point in space. The radiation of heat from a fire or scent from perfume can exhaust itself. To use another of his metaphors, a seed requires nourishment and eventually grows into something more perfect.[16] None of this is true of an intelligible form. Beyond problems of exhaustion and localization, there is also the problem of temporality. Plotinus is not saying that we begin with the first principle and after a series of steps arrive at the world as we know it. On the contrary, he warns (*EN* 5.1.6): "When we are discussing eternal realities we must not let coming into being in time be an obstacle to our thought." The world as we know it has always existed and will always exist; what the procession of things from the first principle allows us to see is the order and structure of the world.

Let us return to the relation between triangularity and an individual triangle. It is not that triangularity overflows into shapes on a blackboard but that its perfection is constitutive of those shapes. This is true even though it takes no action of its own and is unaffected by anything that happens outside it. Although triangularity is present in every triangle, it is not dispersed or diffused. How then can it be described as active? How, as Plotinus puts it, can the first principle continue to bestow gifts just by being what it is? The

---

[14] Aristotle, *Metaphysics* 1048b18–34.
[15] See, for example, *EN* 6.4.7.
[16] For references to seeds, see *EN* 3.37, 5.9.6.

answer is that Plotinus' understanding of activity is derived from *Republic* 7, not *Metaphysics* 9.

A cause is always active relative to its effect in the sense that the effect derives from and is understood through its cause. Just as snow and fire take no specific steps to cool or warm the things around them, according to Plotinus, the first principle takes no specific steps to bring about emanation. To be active in the intelligible realm is not to perform a task but to exhibit perfection. Insofar as the effect is a manifestation of this perfection, it is a trace or copy of the cause and wholly dependent on the cause. Recall that according to *Republic* 517, goodness produces and controls truth and intelligence. Obviously it cannot produce or control anything in a literal sense. It is rather that truth and intelligence presuppose goodness and would have no reality of their own without it. This is what enables Plato to say that goodness is superior to them and controls them.

Aristotle objected that Platonic forms affect nothing and for that reason are a senseless duplication of the world around us. So persuasive was this argument that in later ages many of those who accepted emanation insisted that God had to be doing something and therefore that God thinks.[17] Influential as this view may be for the history of philosophy, we must be careful not to read it into Plotinus. The first principle affects things for the simple reason that without it nothing would have any degree of unity or perfection and thus nothing would exist. But the first principle does not think, because it is prior to thought, as that from which thought proceeds.[18] I have more to say on this issue later in the chapter.

---

[17] See, for example, Alfarabl, *Al-Madīna* 1.1.6–7.

[18] *EN* 3.9.9, 5.6.2. According to Rist, *Plotinus, The Road to Reality*, pp. 38–51, there are grounds for saying that the first principle has a unique form of self-directed awareness, for example, *EN* 5.4.2. But Armstrong (*The Cambridge History of Later Greek and Early Medieval Philosophy*, pp. 238–39) argues that the purpose of such passages is to prevent the reader from thinking that the first principle is less than intellect rather than to suggest that it is an intellect.

For the present, it is best to conclude that the relation between the first principle and thought is essentially the same as that between goodness and intelligence in Plato's *Republic*. Just as goodness determines the nature of intelligence without manifesting it, so the first principle determines the nature of thought without being engaged in it.

## II

Thus far we have investigated Plotinus' view of form and the causality associated with it. But there is more to his view of the universe than form – in particular, matter and the principle of difference or differentiation. Plotinus' view of matter is difficult to assess for a number of reasons. Again he uses metaphors, and in so doing raises the question of what is to be taken literally and what not. In some cases, he expresses himself by asking questions rather than stating arguments. Like Maimonides, he feels free to tailor different arguments to different sets of opponents. Finally, it is not always clear whether he is talking about intelligible matter or sensible.

We saw that for Plato, the receptacle is not a cause in the Aristotelian sense of the term. Rather than that *out* of which a thing comes to be, it is that *in* which copies of the forms are represented. In our terms, it is a medium rather than a substratum. As such, the receptacle does not change as different qualities pass through it: although it reflects them, it does not *become* them.[19] By Plato's admission (*Timaeus* 51a), its participation in the intelligible order is puzzling and difficult to understand. Rather than a scientific principle known by the light of reason, it is apprehended by what Plato calls a bastard or an illegitimate reason.[20]

---

[19] *Timaeus* 50b–c.
[20] *Timaeus* 52b.

There is little doubt that Plotinus accepts the broad outlines of this position. Matter (*hulē*) is impassive in that it is neither changed nor modified. In a passage that clearly refers to Aristotle (*EN* 3.6.9), Plotinus says that when hot and cold are present in it, it undergoes no change of temperature. It is immune to the things that pass through it just as a mirror is immune to the images that bounce off it. Nothing penetrates it and nothing remains. To speak of matter as changing, Plotinus argues (*EN* 3.6.10), is to speak of it as not being matter at all. Like Plato, he claims that matter's participation in the intelligible order is false or deceiving.[21] Although it may seem to take on distinct qualities like hot or cold, Plotinus assures us that this is mere appearance. In his words (*EN* 2.4.5), it is no better than a decorated corpse completely separate from being.[22] If by evil we mean something that is not subject to modification by the good, in fact something that is not subject to modification at all, then matter for Plotinus is ultimate and irredeemable evil.[23]

Because the good is the source being, matter is sometimes called nonbeing (*to mē on*).[24] This does not mean that it is totally unreal and plays no part in a description of the world. That sense of nonbeing was excluded by Parmenides and rejected in Plato's *Sophist*.[25] Rather Plotinus takes nonbeing to mean "the part of otherness which is opposed to the things which in the full and proper sense exist, that is to say rational formative principles."[26] The problem is that although matter may be evil, ugly, and false, part of the world we inhabit is evil, ugly, and false, from which it follows that the

---

[21] *EN* 3.6.11.

[22] *EN* 2.5.5.

[23] *EN* 3.6.11.

[24] *EN* 2.4.16. Also see 1.8.3, 3.9.3

[25] *Sophist* 237b–239c.

[26] *EN* 2.4.16. Cf. *Sophist* 258d–e, where the Stranger says that the nature of the different has existence and is parceled out over the whole field of existent things. Also see 1.8.6, where, against Aristotle, Plotinus says that matter is the contrary of substance.

world we inhabit would not exist if matter did not exist.[27] In that sense, matter functions as a cause or principle of the generated realm.[28]

Still, the existence of matter is paradoxical. After defining it as the part of otherness opposed to things which exist in the proper sense, Plotinus says that it enjoys a certain kind of existence (*ti on*) of its own. At *EN* 3.6.6, he defines it as "the being of things that do not exist." Or more fully (*EN* 2.5.5):

> So it is actually a phantasm [*eidōlon*]: so it is actually a falsity: this is the same as "that which is truly a falsity"; this is "what is really unreal." That, then, which has its truth in nonexistence [*en tō mē onti*]. If, then, it must exist it must actually not exist, so that, having gone out of true being, it may have its being in non-being.

Clearly there is a problem. You can say that what stands in opposition to reason is nothing. To use one of Plotinus' favorite analogies, matter is to reason what darkness is to the eye.[29] Yet this cannot be the end of the story. In a system that relies on the metaphor of light, darkness plays an important role. According to *EN* 1.8.7, if everything proceeds from the first principle, there must be a last item in the series. Therefore, it is necessary that matter exist even though it does not possess anything of the goodness of its source. Matter, then, is an enigma: both nothing and a diminished something, both darkness and a surface that reflects light.

If Plotinus is right, matter cannot be grasped with the eye, has no odor, flavor, or corporeality. In fact, it can only be grasped by a mental process.[30] Not surprisingly, he invokes Plato's idea of a bastard reason.[31] But again a problem arises. After mentioning bastard

[27] *EN* 1.8.7.
[28] *EN* 3.6.14.
[29] See, for example, *EN* 5.1.2.
[30] *EN* 2.4.12.
[31] *EN* 2.4.4.10.

reason, Plotinus claims that to think about matter is different from not thinking at all. Just as there is a sense in which the eye *can* see darkness as part of the visual field, so the mind can think about matter even though it has no form or determination.

Where Plotinus differs from Plato is on the origin of matter.[32] Whereas Plato has two principles, Reason and Necessity, Plotinus has only one. Accordingly, Plotinus presents several arguments for why matter is generated or dependent on the first principle. The first, which occurs at *EN* 2.4.2, maintains that if it is *un*generated, the first principles of the universe would be multiplex and related by chance. Suppose there are two ultimate or ungenerated principles. How would we explain their interaction? The only way would be to say that they are dependent on a more inclusive principle that accounts for how they relate to one another. But no such principle exists. Therefore, the supposed interaction of the two ultimate principles is incoherent. It follows that if, per impossible, there were such interaction, it would be left to chance, which in this context is another name for absurdity. A similar argument can be found in the treatise against the Gnostics (*EN* 2.9.12). Matter is evil. Therefore, if matter were ungenerated, one of the first principles would be evil.

If matter has any reality, it must derive it from something – eventually from the first principle because all of reality derives from the first principle. I say *to the degree that it has any reality* because we have seen that its status is problematic. If we stress that matter is irredeemably evil, we will be led to think that it has no reality

---

[32] On this issue, I am guided by and indebted to Denis O'Brien, "Plotinus and the Gnostics on the Generation of Matter," *Neoplatonism and Early Christian Thought*, ed. H. J. Blumenthal and R. A. Markus, pp. 108–23; and "Plotinus on Matter and Evil," *CCP*, pp. 171–95. For other points of view, see H. R. Schwyzer, "Zu Plotins Deutung der sogenanntenplatonischen Materie," in *Zetesis. Festschrift E. de Strijcker*, pp. 266–80; and Kevin Corrigan, "Is There More Than One Generation of Matter in the Enneads?" *Phronesis* 21 (1986): 167–81. For O'Brien's reply, see *Plotinus on the Origin of Matter*. For others who accept the generation of matter in Plotinus, see Armstrong, *The Cambridge History*, p. 256, and Rist, *Plotinus*, pp. 117–19.

and thus cannot be generated by anything. On this reading, it is the point where the light that emanates from the first principle runs out. This would not give it the status of a separate principle but rather that which is opposed to principle. If we stress that the existence of the first item in a series implies the existence of a last, the generation of matter by the first principle is inescapable.

To be sure, matter, at least sensible matter, cannot be generated immediately. From the first principle we get intelligence, and from intelligence soul. By some accounts, sensible matter is generated by a "partial" or vegetative soul.[33] The important point, however, is that it is generated at all and does not exist in its own right. The first principle does not shape it, confront it, or exist alongside it. If matter existed in its own right, the first principle would be limited, or, to use Plotinus' expression, "walled off from matter."[34] Again we reach absurdity because nothing can limit the first principle, especially something that is completely lacking in perfection. This insight, as Denis O'Brien argues, is supported by the image of a light that *becomes* darkness as it falls away from the source rather than a light that is surrounded by darkness that exists independently of the light.[35] If that is true, instead of a Demiurge who imposes form on matter, the first principle is just that: a principle to which all of reality, including matter, owes its existence. It is in that form that Maimonides encounters the theory of emanation, not a form that has matter existing alongside God as a second principle or partner.

It bears repeating that Plotinus does not always express himself in a way that allows one to formulate doctrines. The point is that unlike Plato and Aristotle, he refuses to take matter as a given and raises the question of its origin. The issue then becomes: From a first principle that is one and wholly good, how do we get to a world that contains evil, ugliness, and falsity? The metaphor of a

[33] *EN* 3.9.3, 3.4.1.
[34] *EN* 2.9.3.
[35] O'Brien, *Plotinus on the Origin*, p. 20. The passage in question is *EN* 4.3.9.

light that eventually runs out is helpful to the degree that it puts earthly matter at the opposite end of the scale from God. But like most metaphors, its effectiveness is limited. If the first principle is infinite and limited by nothing, why does the light run out at all? Why does an infinite cause not give rise to an infinite effect? Clearly something more must be involved.

III

Plotinus' answer lies in a claim we have already encountered: what is prior to all things cannot *be* any of them: what produces the world of sense cannot be sensible, what produces thought cannot think, what produces being cannot be, and, more important, what produces multiplicity cannot be multiplex.[36] So unlike Aristotle, Plotinus does not think a cause must have the property it gives. According to *EN* 6.7.17: "There is no necessity for anyone to have what he gives, but in this kind of situation one must consider that the giver is greater, and that which is given is less than the giver; for that is how coming to be is among the real beings."[37] Because the cause is simpler than the effect, it is *better* than the effect, which means that the effect contains things not found in the cause. If the cause had the property it gives, both the cause and the effect would have to get that property from something else: a second cause superior to both.

Following Cristina D'Ancona Costa, I suggest that behind Plotinus' view of causality is the problem of self-predication.[38] According to the Third Man Argument of the *Parmenides*, if beauty is beautiful, and all beautiful things need a form that makes them so, then all beautiful things *and* beauty would need another form, and so on ad infinitum. Mindful of these objections, Plotinus answers that the

---

[36] *EN* 5.2.1, 5.3.16.
[37] Cf. Proclus, *Elements of Theology*, prop. 18.
[38] D'Ancona Costa, "The Causality of the First Principle," *CCP*, p. 72.

form of *F* is what generates it, not what has it. Once that is granted, the emergence of multiplicity from unity is not a paradox but an inevitable feature of the causal process. The priority of the cause to the effect requires that the effect is an articulation of the cause in just the way that various kinds of triangle are articulations of triangularity. The issue, then, is not that the first principle is limited but that once the perfection of the first principle manifests itself in the generation of offspring, complexity and multiplicity are inevitable.

Intriguing as this answer is, it raises several questions of its own. Fire, one of Plotinus' favorite examples, does resemble its effect. As we saw, Plotinus follows Plato in talking about participation and describing the effect as a trace or image of its cause. Although we are once again in the realm of metaphor, it is hard to avoid the conclusion that for Plotinus causality must involve some sort of resemblance even if it is not the simple kind that occurs when an attribute is passed from one thing to another. Both the essence of triangularity and an instance of it are intelligible: one because it tells us what it is to be a triangle, the other because it manifests it. There is a difference in the *way* they are intelligible. The intelligibility of the essence is internal to it, whereas that of the instance is derivative. So although there is a resemblance between them, it is not like that which holds between one triangle and another. Not only is the resemblance between the essence and an instance asymmetrical, it is constitutive of the copy because the copy would be nothing without it. It follows that although it makes sense to say that the effect resembles the cause, it is still true that the cause is simpler and more perfect than the effect.

This is best seen in the relation between the first principle and intellect. That intellect is an image of the first principle and retains some of its goodness Plotinus has no doubt.[39] As we saw, the first principle does not think, so there is no question of passing an

---

[39] *EN* 5.1.7.

attribute to something that does. According to *EN* 5.1.6, nothing can come from the first principle except that which is next in respect of perfection. The assumption at work here is that because the first principle is simple, it can produce only one effect. Anything else would imply that it gives something to *A* that it withholds from *B*, implying complexity in the source. This doctrine is reiterated at *EN* 5.3.15, when Plotinus grants that from the perfection of the first principle, it is possible for one thing to proceed.

Even if this is true, the effect is derived from the cause and cannot have the same degree of perfection as the cause. Thus, the effect, although one, must exhibit some degree of complexity. At the most fundamental level, it is the same as itself and different from what produced it.[40] We can see this another way if we take into account that what emerges from the first principle is intellect. When intellect contemplates the first principle, it realizes that it needs the first principle if it is going to have any reality of its own.[41] In striving to possess the unity of the first principle, it falls short, and in so doing a distinction arises between thought and its object. Once we have such a distinction, we no longer have radical simplicity.

The *Letter Concerning Divine Science* sheds more light on this doctrine by claiming that although the first principle is the cause of all things, it does not generate them one after another – like a chicken laying eggs.[42] Rather, the first principle generates all things *as though they were one* because the effect it produces serves as a secondary cause for the production of other things: the perfection embodied in the first principle produces something else, which in turn produces something else, until we get to the world as we know it. The principle at work here – one cause, one effect – will become a bone of contention when Maimonides takes up the subject

---

[40] *EN* 5.3.15.
[41] *EN* 5.1.7, 5.3.11.
[42] *Letter Concerning Divine Science* 139–49 (*The Works of Plotinus*, Henry and Schwyzer), p. 327.

of emanation in Book Two of the *Guide*. How, Maimonides asks, can a single cause ever produce a complex world? For now the answer is that each effect dilutes the perfection of its cause so that by the time we reach the sensible world, evil, ugliness, and falsity are unavoidable

## IV

It is easy to see why some aspects of Plotinus' philosophy are not only compatible with monotheism but became definitive of it. The dualism of the pagan world has been replaced by the dependence of all things on a common source. Any hint of struggle between this source and something else has been eliminated. So has any suggestion that the source acts like a human being. The way to approach it is to turn away from the temporal and focus on the eternal.

Still, the fit between biblical religion and Plotinian Neoplatonism is far from perfect. The Bible says that God called the world into existence not that it proceeded from God as heat proceeds from a fire. Even if we agree that there is no second principle or preexistent matter to contend with, we must decide whether the world proceeds *from* God or is a separate thing created *by* God. Unless one maintains strict adherence to the "prior to *F*, therefore not *F*" principle, any talk of procession from God will suggest that the essence of God is manifested in the world, making it difficult to avoid pantheism.[43] The pantheist objection receives additional support from the many passages where Plotinus claims that the first principle contains all things, is in all things, or *is* all things.[44] This language should not worry us too much, however. Plotinus' language can easily be understood to mean that the world "is derived from" the

[43] On this point, see *EN* 6.5.12, cited by Armstrong in "Emanation," p. 62, n. 2.
[44] *EN* 4.5.7, 5.3.15, 5.5.9, 6.8.18, 6.5.1. For further discussion, see John Bussanich, "Plotinus' Metaphysics of the One," *CCP*, pp. 57–63.

first principle or that the first principle "is responsible for" the world. Because his understanding of responsibility implies that the cause is simpler and more perfect than the effect, he can always claim that the first principle and its offspring are ontologically distinct.

Beyond their distinctness, there is the general point that, as Gilson remarks, what people refer to as the pantheism of Plotinus is an illusion brought on by the interplay of two inconsistent doctrines.[45] For a Christian thinker like Aquinas, the world owes its being to God because God's being is necessary and absolute. In this scheme, the cause gives something of itself to the effect. In Plotinus' scheme, the cause cannot give something of itself to the effect or else it would be the effect. So there is no possibility of saying that all of reality is one thing or that a single nature is everywhere present. To repeat: the first principle is not all things but the generator of all things. Even so, some Christians felt uncomfortable with Plotinus and held that unlike the persons of the trinity, who emerged from the essence of God and are in some sense still a part of that essence, the world was created *ex nihilo*.[46]

That takes us back to the question of how multiplicity can arise from unity. Plotinus' position stands or falls with the "prior to $F$, therefore not $F$" principle. Unfortunately, the tendency to insist that the cause must give something of itself to the effect runs deep. According to E. R. Dodds, Plotinus himself comes close to admitting that you cannot get complexity from simplicity unless complexity is already there to some degree.[47] If the first principle is the source of all things, must it not contain the seed of multiplicity? If the answer is yes, the unity of the first principle is compromised. If no, the emergence of multiplicity will begin to seem mysterious.

---

[45] Gilson, *Being*, p. 23.

[46] For examples and further discussion, see Wolfson, *SHPR*, Vol. 1, pp. 199–201.

[47] E. R. Dodds, *Proclus: The Elements of Theology*, p. 259. The passage in question is *EN* 6.5.9.

One does not have to read far in the history of philosophy to see that many of the Neoplatonists who came after Plotinus tried to ease the severity of the transition from unity to multiplicity by increasing the number of hypostases. Proclus introduces a seemingly endless array of gods or henads.[48] Alfarabi and Avicenna introduce ten intelligences and nine primary spheres separating God from earthly matter. But these solutions also raise problems. Even if there are a million hypostases, the question of how multiplicity can arise from unity cannot be avoided. One reason Plotinus warns against the multiplication of hypostases and insists that intellect proceeds from the first principle without intermediaries is that he thought he had answered it: because the first principle is not multiple, whatever comes after it must be.[49] If this is true, the emergence of multiplicity from unity is immediate and necessary, so no other hypostasis is needed. As we will see in another chapter, the introduction of additional hypostases does not solve the problem of multiplicity and raises further problems of its own.

The most serious problem in trying to reconcile Plotinus with biblical religion has to do with volition. Is the first principle an agent who acts for a purpose or merely a cause from which the world proceeds? This is another way of asking whether it makes sense to say that the first principle is free. Again we face the difficulty of applying language to an ineffable reality removed from ordinary experience. At an elementary level, the first principle is not like Plato's Demiurge, who plans what he is going to do and promises the created gods the he will not destroy them. For Plotinus, the ability to choose between alternatives implies indecision and is a sign of deficiency.[50] If the first principle had to decide whether to produce this as opposed to that, its production and therefore its power would be limited. There is then no question of

[48] *Elements*, prop. 113–27.
[49] *EN* 2.9.1, 5.1.6.
[50] Also see *EN* 3.2.1, 5.8.12, 6.8.8.

its withholding production or producing only a portion of what it is capable of making: everything that can be produced is produced.[51] Because only one result is possible, Plotinus insists that there is no room for foresight or decision. Nor is there any possibility of wanting something other than what it has made; any kind of desire or inclination is ruled out from the beginning.[52]

Still, it would be a mistake to think that the first principle is subject to external constraint. Because it is not the effect of a prior cause, nothing else can influence it or subvert it. In that respect, it can be described as free. But the freedom it has does not extend to the ability to start, stop, or guide the production of offspring – all of that takes place by necessity. In some places, Plotinus goes so far as to deny that the first principle is master of himself lest we think that there is a part of his nature over which he must exercise control.[53]

The picture becomes more complicated at *EN* 6.8.13, where Plotinus permits a temporary departure from "correct thinking" and employs expressions that he says must be taken in the sense of "as if" (*hoion*). There he allows the claim that the first principle is master of himself on the grounds that he wills himself to be and has his being within his own power. If that is true, not only does he will himself to be, he acts according to his will. This passage has led some to argue that it is wrong to say that the first principle acts by necessity.[54] Because the only necessity Plotinus allows comes from

---

[51] *EN* 4.8.6.
[52] *EN* 5.1.6.
[53] *EN* 6.8.12.
[54] The most distinguished representative of this school is J. M. Rist, *Plotinus*, pp. 66–83. According to Rist, although it is wrong to say that the will of the first principle is responsible for its activity, it is closer to the truth to say that the will is its activity. Thus, the first principle wills what it is and is what it wills. It is true that what emanates from the first principle does so necessarily. If we ask why, Rist's answer (p. 82) is that the first principle wills it. If so, the first principle as well as its products derive from its will. The question is what Rist means by *will*. If we take Maimonides' meaning – to will or not will – it would follow that the first principle and its products could be different from what they are, which is clearly false. If we do not take this meaning,

within, it is part of the will rather than something alien to it. According to a compatibilist conception of behavior, this is not contrary to freedom but the essence of it.

The problem is that the ascription of will to the first principle is not Plotinus' preferred way of speaking. He is not saying that the first principle has a will but that "*if* [my emphasis] we were to grant activities to him, and ascribe his activities to what we might call his will," we will be led to the conclusion that his being and his will are identical. The conditional nature of this claim is important. Although the first principle is active, there is no basis for thinking that it undertakes action in the way a human agent does. We saw that its offspring result not from what it does but simply from what it is. If we wish to emphasize its independence from everything else, we can say that it wills itself to be what it is, but this does not mean it exercises volition as normally understood.

What, then, is volition? We saw that Maimonides characterizes the Aristotelian view of creation in terms of divine volition and that there is a precedent for this in Avicenna. But although freedom from external constraint is a necessary condition for choice, both Alghazali and Maimonides argue that it is not sufficient. For them, compatibilism is false. A God who can only will what the necessity of his own causation requires is not free. Thus, Maimonides argues (*GP* 2.18, p. 301), the true reality of the will is the ability to will or not will – exactly what Plotinus denies to the first principle. For Maimonides, the test of whether something exercises free will is whether it can give existence to something that did not previously have it. We saw, however, that the giving of existence in this sense is not an issue for Plotinus, so that the attribution of volition in the sense in which Alghazali and Maimonides understand it is groundless.

Maimonides (*GP* 2.21) argues in effect that it makes no sense to call someone who adopts Plotinus' position a voluntarist. I discuss *GP* 2.21 in more detail in the next chapter.

V

As already indicated, the theory of emanant causality came to Maimonides through Alfarabi and Avicenna. In a chapter that he himself calls provisional, Maimonides praises emanation on the grounds that it provides us with a type of causality that does not involve physical contact (*GP* 2.12, p. 279):

> It has been said that the world derives from the overflow [*fayḍ*] of God and that He has caused to overflow to it everything in it that is produced in time. In the same way it is said that He caused His knowledge to overflow to the prophets. The meaning of all this is that these actions are the action of one who is not a body. And it is His action that is called overflow.

He goes on to say that nothing is a more fitting metaphor for metaphysical causation than the term *overflow*. Like Plotinus, he recognizes that this is only a metaphor, because the overflowing of a fountain is a mechanical process that occurs in space and time. The passage continues, "We are not capable of finding the true reality of a term that would correspond to the true reality of the notion. For the mental representation [*taṣawwur*] of the action of one who is separate from matter is very difficult."

*GP* 2–12 is meant to show that when it comes to the heavenly realm, the opinions of the philosophers agree with the Law: where one speaks of spheres and intelligences, the other speaks of angels. Maimonides indicates there is room for doubt as to how many spheres there are and whether the spheres of Mercury and Venus are above or below that of the sun. A question raised earlier (*GP* 186, pp. 185–86) as to whether spheres have an intellect that allows them to represent things to themselves is resolved in the affirmative (*GP* 2.4, p. 256). So the heavenly realm contains both embodied and disembodied intelligences, although the bodies in question are composed of heavenly rather than earthly matter. Still, agreement on the existence of heavenly creatures does not imply agreement on their generation. Even before the discussion of creation is introduced (*GP* 2.6, p. 265), Maimonides indicates that he does not believe the spheres and intelligences came to exist by a process of necessary emanation but that they were created.

His ambivalence toward emanation can also be seen in the passage from *GP* 2.12 quoted earlier. Instead of indicating unqualified acceptance, he puts a certain amount of distance between himself and the theory he is describing by claiming: "It has been said that. . . . " He also indicates that one of the dangers of emanation is that it leads a person to think that the stars act at a distance and thus paves the way for astrology (*GP* 2.12, p. 280).

Maimonides' chief objection to the theory of emanation is that although it may be able to account for *a* world, it cannot account for particular features of this one. If God did not take specific action to create the world, and every effect follows necessarily from its cause, why are there things for which there is no scientific explanation? It should be understood that we are not asking about trivial features of the earthly realm – Why did this leaf fall before that one? – but about the movement and diversity of things in the heavenly realm, things that do not exhibit signs of decay and are thought to be close to God. It is to the subject of particularity that we now turn.

# 5

# Particularity

W E HAVE ALREADY ENCOUNTERED THE ARGUMENT FROM
particularity, the crux of which is that if no reason can
be found for why something is one way rather than another, it
must be the product of a free agent or particularizer (*mukhaṣṣiṣ*)
who made the world as we have it.[1] We can understand the force

[1] Wolfson, *The Philosophy of the Kalam*, pp. 434–52, traces the Kalām version of the
argument to the Asharite theologian al-Juwayni and finds it in two forms: (1) given
that the world was created and contains features that could have been otherwise, it
must have been created by an agent with free will; (2) because the world contains
features that could have been otherwise, it must have been created by an agent with
free will. The latter version is taken up Alghazali and Maimonides, and thus it is the
version I focus on here. For a more detailed account of the argument, see Davidson,
*PEC*, chap. 6. For a recent study of Maimonides' representation of Kalām arguments
for creation, see Michael Schwarz, "Who Were Maimonides' Mutakallimun? Some
Remarks on *Guide of the Perplexed* Part 1 Chapter 73," *Maimonidean Studies* 2 (1991):
159–209, and 3 (1992–3): 143–72. On the accuracy of Maimonides' representation,

of the argument if we return to Aristotle. According to the *Posterior Analytics* (71b14–15), the object of scientific knowledge is most properly that which cannot be otherwise. It follows that if there are things in the world that can be otherwise, they will not be subject to scientific understanding. The alternative is to say they can be understood in terms of choice rather than necessity. Once we have a God who exercises choice, we have the basis for asserting creation *de novo*. In Maimonides' words (*GP* 1.74, p. 218): "There is no difference between your saying someone who particularizes or who makes or who creates or who brings into existence or who creates in time or who purposes the universe."

We saw that for Plotinus, there is no possibility of God's being selective: everything that can be produced is produced. Although proponents of emanation can avoid the question of why the world was created at one moment rather than another by claiming that the production in question is eternal, they cannot avoid similar questions in regard to space. Aristotle was supposed to have shown that an actual infinite is impossible. According to the standard medieval account, the world is enclosed by a sphere of finite dimension. In addition to the question "Why is the sphere this size rather than that?" proponents of emanation faced a host of questions about the location of things in the sphere. Why are fixed stars clustered in one area rather than another? Why are the poles of rotation here rather than there? Why are there nine primary spheres rather than another number? Why do the planets seem to move faster than the fixed stars, change speeds, and reverse direction? Each of these questions asks for a reason for something that seems as if it could be otherwise. If none can be found, we have grounds for believing in particularity.

note Schwarz's conclusion: "And in Maimonides' time it was no less common practice than in the present day to misinterpret slightly the adversary's attitude for the sake of argument."

I

Before taking up the various forms of the argument, it would be helpful to look at the theory of emanation as Maimonides found it, which is to say the theory as its occurs in Alfarabi and Avicenna. The world is eternal and depends for its existence on God. Although God is responsible for everything in the world, the only thing God produces directly is the first intelligence.[2] According to Avicenna, the reason for this is the principle we encountered earlier: a cause that is one and simple can only produce an effect that is one and simple.[3] As long as this is true, God cannot produce the entire world in one act. Rather, God set in motion a chain of causes from which everything eventually proceeds. The chain begins with God's thought, which is perfect and unceasing.[4] In God's awareness of himself, there is no plurality and thus no distinction between thought and its object. From there, the first intelligence is generated. Because the first intelligence is aware of itself *and* God, for the first time we get plurality. Once we have plurality in the cause, it is possible to have plurality in the effect.

Unlike Alfarabi, Avicenna accounts for the plurality of the first intelligence by invoking the distinction between necessary and possible existence. Although the first generated intelligence is one, there are three ways we can view its thought: (1) it can reflect on its source (God), whose existence is necessary; (2) it can reflect on

---

[2] Alfarabi, *Al-Madīna* 2.3.1–10, pp. 101–105; Avicenna, *Al-Shifā'* 9.4.406–407.

[3] Avicenna, *Al-Shifā'* 9.4.405–406; cf. Alghazali, *Incoherence* 3.34, p. 65. For emanation in Avicenna, see Herbert Davidson, "The Active Intellect in the *Cuzari* and Hallevi's Theory of Causality," *Revue des Etudes Juives 131* (*1972*): 351–57; Barry Kogan, "Averroes and the Theory of Emanation," *Medieval Studies* 43 (1981): 384–87; Parviz Morewedge, *The Metaphysics of Avicenna*, pp. 264–78. For the history of the "one cause, one effect" principle, see Arthur Hyman, "From What Is One and Simple Only What Is One and Simple Can Come to Be," in *Neoplatonism and Jewish Thought*, edited by Lenn Goodman, pp. 111–35.

[4] Recall that for Plotinus, emanation is the result of the infinite perfection of the first principle, not the fact that it thinks.

itself as a being necessitated by its source; (3) it can reflect on itself as a being whose existence apart from its source is possible rather than necessary. In keeping with the "one cause, one effect" principle, each kind of reflection results in a separate hypostasis, with the noblest kind producing the noblest kind of effect. From (1) we get the second generated intelligence, which is a purely intellectual being; from (2) the soul of the outermost celestial sphere; from (3) the body of the outermost celestial sphere.[5]

This process continues until we get the intelligences and nine primary spheres that constitute the standard picture of medieval cosmology.[6] As in Plotinus, each thing receives a measure of perfection from what comes before it and passes a smaller measure to what comes after. By the time we get to the tenth intelligence or active intellect, the degree of perfection is so slight that no additional intelligences or spheres are generated. Instead we get the forms that provide structure to the sublunar realm and, together with the motion of the heavenly spheres, the matter of the sublunar realm.[7] Ultimately the complexity of the world arises from the fact that no being other than God is necessary in itself and can reflect on itself as God does. But, Avicenna would insist, the "one cause, one effect" principle is still preserved because the effect of God's reflection on himself is only a single thing.

From a scientific standpoint, the advantage of this scheme is that we can take anything in heaven or earth and assign it a place in a causal sequence that explains both the origin of the world and its structure. There are no breaks in which causal connection is abandoned in favor of volition. The problem is that if causal connection is the only form of intelligibility, there is no room for

---

[5] Tripartite emanation is explained at *Al-Shifā'* 9.4, p. 406; cf. Alghazali, *Incoherence* 3.43–4, pp. 68–69.

[6] The existence of a ninth or outermost sphere was debated. See Grant, *Planets, Stars, and Orbs*, pp. 322–23.

[7] *Al-Shifā'* 9.4, pp. 410–11.

contingency as Maimonides understands it: something that exists but does not have to. According to Avicenna, created things are possible in themselves but necessary with respect to their causes.[8] Because the ultimate cause is God, who exists by necessity, possibility arises only when we consider finite things in isolation. As a part of nature, everything is destined to come into existence at a given point and go out at a given point. That is why Maimonides claims that, according to this view, even something as simple as a fly's wing or a worm's foot could not be otherwise.[9]

Avicenna's scheme was subjected to harsh criticism by Alghazali, who argued that it reveals the depths of absurdity into which philosophy can sink.[10] It is clear, for example, that although God is simple, the first intelligence is not. In Avicenna's view, it is triune, having three distinct thoughts. Alghazali objects that despite Avicenna's intention, God is the cause of plurality. Strict adherence to the "one cause, one effect" principle would mean that the first intelligence is also simple and thinks only of itself. If this were so, it could not be the cause of a celestial sphere, which is a composite of body and soul. Aside from the anomaly of having one thing, the first intelligence, be the cause of *both* the form and the matter of the celestial sphere, there is the problem of how to account for the size of the sphere. What principle, Alghazali asks, determines that it is this size rather than another?

Finally, there is the question of why, at each stage of the process, we get another triad. Consider the second intelligence. Why should it not be aware of four or five things: God, the first intelligence as necessary with respect to its cause, the first intelligence as possible, itself as necessary with respect to its cause, and itself as possible? If each thought gives rise to a separate hypostasis, then considering

---

[8] For further discussion of this point, as well as Avicenna's metaphysics in general, see Lenn E. Goodman, *Avicenna*, chap. 2, esp. pp. 80–83.

[9] *GP* 2.22, p. 319.

[10] Alghazali, *Incoherence* 3.48–80, pp. 69–78.

the chain of intelligences, the heavenly realm should contain many more entities than the philosophers think it does.

## II

The argument from particularity took many forms, not all of which Maimonides accepted. In its most extreme form, it was coupled with atomism and occasionalism, both of which deny the existence of natural causation. According to Maimonides (*GP* 1.73), various spokesmen for the Mutakallimun denied the existence of essential natures and believed instead that every material thing is an aggregate of minute particles exactly like one another. What distinguishes a piece of black granite from a piece of white granite is that God created the atoms of one with the accident blackness and the atoms of the other with the accident whiteness. Because all atoms are alike in themselves, however, and differ only according to the accidents that inhere in them, there is nothing in one group that makes it more suitable for exhibiting this color rather than that. Thus, every assignment of color, taste, and smell or humanity, sensation, and rationality is arbitrary. And because no accident lasts for more than a single instant of time, the assignment of accidents to atoms must be repeated constantly. In the last analysis, the only cause for why this is black and that white is the will of God.

From this view of the world, the Mutakallimun devised what Maimonides calls the affirmation of admissibility (*tajwīz*). Anything the mind can imagine, that is, anything free of contraction, is admissible in the sense that God could make it so. Hence: "Should a human individual, for instance, have the size of a big mountain having many summits overtopping the air, or should there exist an elephant having the size of a flea, or a flea having the size of an elephant – all such differences would be admissible from the point of view of the intellect" (*GP* 1.73, p. 206). If they are admissible, the fact that elephants are larger than fleas has to be explained. Because there is nothing inherent in either one to serve as the basis for an explanation, we are again left with arbitrariness. In the end, anything other than the assertion of logical necessity or the denial of logical contradiction turns out to be arbitrary.

Maimonides rejects atomism and the supposition that anything the mind can imagine is possible. In regard to the latter, he argues that because the imagination can only apprehend material things or material forces, it is opposed to the intellect and should not be trusted on such points.[11] Many things that can be conceived by the mind cannot be pictured by the imagination. By the same token, some things that the imagination regards as necessary, for example, that God is material, are impossible from the standpoint of the mind. More important is the fact that Maimonides accepts natural causation when an explanation can be found and refers to God's will only when one cannot. So the idea that the world is overrun with arbitrariness is for him nonsense. We will see, however, that he still accepts a version of the argument from particularity.

In *The Incoherence of the Philosophers*, Alghazali mentions the arbitrariness of this being black and that white in a preliminary stage of the discussion but later abandons it in favor of arguments dealing with the world as a whole. He presents his case as a dialogue between the proponents of eternity and proponents of creation *de novo*. It begins with the familiar objection: Why did God not create the world sooner rather than later?[12] According to the first argument for eternity, if God is a sufficient cause for the existence of the world, there cannot be any lack of power, purpose, or nature that would distinguish one moment of creation from the next. Nor can there be a change in God. Alghazali's answer is that the world was created by an eternal will that decreed its existence at a

---

[11] *GP* 1.73, pp. 209–11.
[12] *Incoherence* 1.9, p. 14.

particular time. To the objection that a sufficient cause cannot delay its effect, he answers by invoking the principle of delayed effect: just as a man can announce that he intends to divorce his wife and not have the divorce take hold until later, so God can intend to create the world but delay the act of creation.

The second argument for eternity is that a thing cannot be distinguished from something exactly like it except by an act of will. Although the proponents of eternity are familiar with the Kalām argument that the existence of white here and black there is as arbitrary as the creation of the world at one point rather than another, Alghazali portrays them as being unconvinced by this objection. For them, an act of will also requires an explanation: If God chose this rather than that, why was his will drawn one way rather than the other? For proponents of eternity, invoking the will of God does not solve the problem but only puts it off.

Alghazali responds by saying that the essence of the will is just a faculty capable of differentiating between similar things. Unless this were true, power alone would be sufficient to explain the world. But power is indifferent to black-white, now-then, or any other pair of contraries. So the problem of creation revolves around two questions: (1) is a choice between exactly similar things conceivable? and (2) does the world contain features for which no rational explanation can be found?

In answer to the first question, the proponents of eternity say that a choice between absolutely similar things makes no sense, for it implies that neither thing can be distinguished from the other. In fact, absolute similarity never occurs, because even two black beads can be distinguished spatially or temporally. If they were similar in every respect, they would be one rather than two. It follows that if we grant they are two, and if the will prefers one to the other, there must be some basis for the choice. Imagine a thirsty person looking at two glasses of water. If she chooses one, it could only be because she thought it better, lighter, or closer than the alternative.

Unless this were true, "differentiating something from its like is in no sense conceivable."[13]

But, Alghazali, points out, it *is* possible to imagine a choice between exactly similar things. To stay with the water example, suppose that the two glasses do not differ in respect of quality, weight, or distance. Suppose that every other feature is also similar and that differences in space or time balance each other out. Is it not true that a thirsty person would pick one glass arbitrarily rather than die? If it is, there must be a faculty that allows her to do so, and this can only be the will.

As for the second argument, Alghazali shifts from specific things in the world to the structure of the world itself. Although we can imagine the world being larger or smaller than it is, he concedes that the explanation for the actual size may elude us. A bigger or smaller world would mean a different number of heavenly bodies and could result in a structure with other deficiencies as well. But, he continues, there is not and can never be an explanation for why the outermost sphere of the universe rotates around a particular set of poles. The philosophers themselves admit that a heavenly sphere is a simple nature, all of whose points are similar by virtue of being equidistant from the center. If one point differed from another, the universe might as well be enclosed by a quadrilateral shape rather than a spherical one. Thus, anything that can be said on behalf of one set of poles can be said on behalf of an infinite number of others.

A similar argument is presented in regard to the direction of the spheres. Why does the outermost sphere move from east to west, whereas the sphere of the fixed stars moves from west to east? If one answers that the spheres cannot all move in the same direction or else the motion of the heavenly bodies as seen on earth would be disrupted, he counters by saying that everything we now

---

[13] *Incoherence* 1.44, p. 23.

see could be accounted for if, contrary to what the philosophers believe, the outermost sphere moved from west to east, and the sphere of the fixed stars moved from east to west. In other words, reverse the direction of the spheres, and the same result would be produced. Why, then, should we believe that the current direction of rotation is necessary? If these features of the world were chosen from equally desirable alternatives by an arbitrary will, there is no reason God could not also choose one moment for the world's creation as opposed to another. If so, one of the main arguments on behalf of eternity is invalid.

## III

Maimonides employs a similar version of the argument at *GP* 2.19 and claims it comes close to being a demonstration. The chapter begins with a restatement of Aristotle's position: God exists by necessity, and everything else proceeds from God by a similar necessity. Just as we cannot ask why God exists, we cannot ask why the world exists either. Maimonides' point is that when something cannot be otherwise, the question "Why is it so?" makes no sense. Here as elsewhere he takes this to mean that for Aristotle and his followers, nothing has been freely chosen and thus nothing has come into being for a purpose.[14]

Having indicated that he disagrees with Aristotle, Maimonides goes on to say that he also disagrees with the Mutakallimūn. We saw that in their view, all accidents are chosen arbitrarily, so that there is no difference between a thing's being black as opposed to white or bitter as opposed to sweet. Despite his rejection of this view, Maimonides is honest enough to admit that "there is no doubt that they wished what I wish" (*GP* 2.19, p. 303). I take this to mean that both oppose universal necessity and want to make room for

[14] Cf. *GP* 2.20.

purpose and choice. As we will see, the problem is that by making choice completely arbitrary, the Mutakallimun are also opposed to purpose as Maimonides understands it.

Like Alghazali, Maimonides presents his argument as a dialogue. Everyone agrees that when things possess a common matter, there must be a cause other than the matter to account for their diversity. For things in the sublunar realm, diversity is explained by the presence of the forms of earth, air, fire, and water and the way these elements get mixed and separated in the formation of compounds. From such mixing and separating, things are disposed to receive other forms and thus to individuate themselves. To the question of why the original matter received one of the forms of the elements, Maimonides refers to Aristotle's theory of natural motion: fire is naturally suited to be higher than the others because it is nearer to the celestial sphere; because of their slowness and density, the remaining elements are farther away.

Given the principle that different movements imply different forms, we can conclude that the matter of the celestial spheres is one, because all move in a circular fashion, whereas their specific forms are different, because some rotate from east to west and others rotate from west to east. Because the matter of the stars and planets is fixed in that of the celestial sphere in which they are situated, one type of matter moves because it is carried around by something else whereas the other type moves by itself. This leads Maimonides to conclude that there must be two types of celestial matter (*GP* 2.19, p. 309), one for the star and one for the sphere. Unfortunately, the existence of two types of matter creates problems. How can one type be attached to another and not mix with it? Given that the matter of the sphere is everywhere the same, why are the stars and planets attached to their respective spheres at one point rather than another? And why are certain stretches of the sphere of the fixed stars heavily populated while others are relatively empty?

Beyond these differences, there is the fact that some spheres rotate faster than others. For example, the spheres of the planets rotate faster than the sphere of the fixed stars. To make matters worse, recall that although there are nine primary spheres, there had to be more than forty secondary spheres to account for the motion of the planets. What causes one sphere to receive one form and another to receive a different one? One answer is that God assigned to each sphere a separate identity and particularized the heavens according to his will. But this answer is not available to Aristotle or his followers, because they have to show that the differences can be explained through causal necessity. As Maimonides points out, and as Ross confirms, Aristotle is stuck with facts that do not seem to have any reason or purpose.[15]

It is not just the diversity of the spheres that poses a problem, but also the specifics of their movement. Because each sphere imparts motion to the one below it, it would be natural to suppose that the closer one gets to earth, the slower is the rotation. But experience confirms that this is not the case. As Maimonides observes (*GP* 2.19, p. 307):

> We see that in case of some spheres, the swifter of motion is above the slower; that in the case of others, the slower of motion is above the swifter; and that, again in another case, the motions of the spheres are of equal velocity though one be above the other. There are also other very grave matters if regarded from the point of view these things are as they are in virtue of necessity.

Without causal explanations of these phenomena, there are no grounds for claiming they cannot be otherwise.

In addition to the velocity of celestial motion, there is also the question of its direction. Why does it often appear to reverse itself, with one sphere moving in the opposite direction of the one directly above it? The need for reverse movement, or what Aristotle called

---

[15] *GP* 2.19, p. 307; Ross, *Aristotle's Metaphysics*, p. cxxxviii.

a "counteracting sphere," can be understood if we recognize that the retrograde motion of every planet is unique to it. Thus, the secondary spheres needed to explain the motion of Saturn must be reversed when we start to explain the motion of Jupiter, and Jupiter's reversed when we start to explain the motion of Mars.[16] In all, twenty-two counteracting spheres were needed for Aristotle's system to work. Reverse motion is all the more difficult to explain given the belief that there is no space or vacuum between one sphere and another.[17] Finally, there is the problem of why the fixed stars do not exhibit retrograde motion, the planets do, but the sun and moon, which according to Aristotle are closest to the earth, also do not.

Maimonides considers Aristotle's suggestion that the particularity exhibited by the spheres can be accounted for by the separate intellects, with one intellect assigned to each sphere.[18] He responds by saying that the separate intellects are of no help on this matter because the intellects are not bodies and have no spatial position relative to the sphere with which they are connected. If so, it is hard to see why desire for one intellect would result in motion from east to west at one speed while desire for another would result in motion from west to east at another.

With his usual respect for Aristotle, Maimonides claims that Aristotle himself realized that his account of the heavens is weak and makes reference to "strange and bizarre causes." From a historical standpoint, there is little doubt this is true. In the words of D. R. Dicks:

> We see, then, from this outline of his [Aristotle's] astronomical thought that there was much that he left obscure and many points on which he never arrived at a satisfactory conclusion.

[16] Aristotle, *Metaphysics* 1073b38–1074a5. For further comment, see Grant, *PSO*, pp. 275–77, as well as D. R. Dicks, *Early Greek Astronomy to Aristotle*, pp. 199–201.

[17] *GP* 1.72, p. 184.

[18] Aristotle, *Metaphysics* 1074a14–31.

This remains true however much allowance we may try to make for the facts that the *De Caelo* is not concerned with scientific astronomy, and that this treatise and the *Physics* and *Metaphysics* contain opinions representing different stages of his thought. In several places Aristotle himself emphasizes the difficulty of the subject and the provisional nature of the explanations offered, and warns us not to expect final answers to the problems, and we learn also from Simplicius of Aristotle's doubts as to the validity of the whole theory of planetary movements including his own concept of counteracting spheres.

What Dicks refers to as Aristotle's doubts are a series of passages in *De Caelo* and the *Metaphysics* where Aristotle admits that our ability to observe heavenly bodies is limited, so that in many cases we have no choice but to settle for probable arguments.

At *De Caelo* 287b31–288a2, for example, Aristotle claims: "One should first consider what reason there is for speaking, and also what kind of certainty is looked for, whether human merely or of a more cogent kind. When any one shall succeed in finding proofs of greater precision, gratitude will be due to him for the discovery, but at present we must be content with a probable solution."[19] In Dicks' view, even the idea of a counteracting sphere may have been put forward as "an interesting speculation" rather than a statement of fact.[20]

If we cannot have more than probable arguments, the claim of necessity becomes all the more difficult to sustain. One can always say, as Moses of Narbonne did in response to Maimonides, that our inability to explain heavenly phenomena reveals more about us than it does about them.[21] Granted that Aristotle's account of the heavens leaves much to be desired. Why should we give up on scientific explanation altogether and turn to the will of God? After

---

[19] Cf. *De Caelo* 286a4–7, 291b25–8, 292a14–18; *Metaphysics* 1074a14–16. Also see Simplicius' commentary on *De Caelo*, p. 505.
[20] Dicks, *Early Greek Astronomy*, p. 203.
[21] Moses Narboni, *Commentary on the Guide of the Perplexed* 2.19.

all, Maimonides himself admits that astronomy has made progress since Aristotle's day and holds out the possibility that someone will find a suitable explanation for what seems baffling to him.[22]

Although Maimonides' recognition that someone may come up with a better explanation for planetary motion is genuine, we should not make too much of it. The possibility that someone may find a better explanation than we have now is always present and thus cannot prove any particular theory true or false. More to the point, Maimonides' remark raises the question of what a better explanation would be like. Maimonides was aware that from the standpoint of predictive power, Ptolemy's theory was superior to Aristotle's, and at one point (*GP* 2.24, p. 326) remarks that Ptolemy's account of the path of the moon is accurate to less than a minute. Although someone could improve on this, to the degree that the new theory makes use of epicycles and eccentric orbits, it would raise the same question that Ptolemy's theory raised: how to reconcile epicycles and eccentrics with Aristotle's theory of natural motion?

Citing Ibn Bajja, Maimonides points out that Aristotle's theory asserts that (1) all motion is either from the midpoint of the earth, toward it, or around it and (2) circular motion must proceed around an immovable point. "How," he asks (ibid.), "can one imagine a rolling motion in the heavens or a motion around a center that is not immovable?"[23] Although Maimonides appears to accept

---

[22] A case in point is the eccentricity of the sun, which requires fewer motions than Aristotle's theory and thus represents an advance. On this point, see *GP* 2.11, pp. 273–74, and 2.24, p. 326.

[23] *MT* 1, Basic Laws of the Torah, 3.4. For further discussion of the difference between the *Guide* and *Mishneh Torah*, see Tzvi Langermann, "The True Perplexity: The *Guide of the Perplexed*, Part II, Chapter 24," *PM*, pp. 159–74. It is true as Langermann indicates (p. 168) that an epicycle would not involve a rolling motion unless it were coupled with eccentricity. In answer to this: (1) those epicycles that do involve eccentric orbits are still objectionable, and (2) even without eccentric orbits, epicycles violate the principle that every movement is either from the center of the earth, toward it, or around it. The fact that Maimonides cites Ibn Bajja does not indicate that he is distancing himself from other aspects of Aristotelian natural

epicycles in the *Mishneh Torah*, in this part of the *Guide*, he claims in his own name that epicycles and eccentrics are "outside the bounds of reasoning and opposed to all that has been made clear in natural science."[24] Nor was he alone in saying this. Both Averroes and Aquinas expressed similar doubts.[25]

The problem is that there was no good way to account for the motion of the planets without epicycles. Whereas Maimonides accepts the principles of Aristotelian natural philosophy, he recognizes that Aristotle's astronomy is deeply flawed and that something else is needed. Unfortunately, the main alternative constitutes too radical a break with the part of Aristotle he wants to retain. What do you do when a theory you think rests on questionable principles has great success in predicting the relevant phenomena? As is well known, Maimonides call this "true perplexity" and claims in two places that the purpose of the astronomer is not to tell us the way the spheres truly are but to posit an astronomical system in which it is possible for motion to be circular and uniform and correspond to what we see "regardless of whether or not things are thus in fact."[26]

philosophy. Finally, the fact that later thinkers, especially Gersonides, tried to defend epicycles against the criticisms voiced by Maimonides and Ibn Bajja does not show that Maimonides is willing to accept them. For a more recent statement by Langermann, see "Maimonides and Astronomy: Some Further Reflections," *The Jews and the Sciences in the Middle Ages*, pp. 1–26. For a different view of the difference between the *Guide* and the *Mishneh Torah*, see Kellner, "On the Status of Astronomy and Physics in Maimonides' *Mishneh Torah* and *Guide of the Perplexed*," *British Journal for the History of Science* 24 (1991): 453–63.

[24] As noted earlier (n. 10), Maimonides sides with Ptolemy regarding the eccentricity of the sun. I take this as a preliminary remark showing that Maimonides admires the parsimony of Ptolemy's theory, not that he accepts eccentricity and the rest of Ptolemy's theory. If anything, the advantages of Ptolemy's theory highlight the extent of Maimonides' perplexity. For more on the historical background to Maimonides' perplexity, see A. I. Sabra, "The Andalusian Revolt against Ptolemaic Astronomy," in *Transformation and Tradition in the Sciences*, ed. Everett Mendelsohn, pp. 133–53.

[25] Averroes, *Ibn Rushd's Metaphysics: A Translation with Introduction of Ibn Rushd's Commentary on Aristotle's Metaphysics, Book Lam*, trans. C. Genequand, 1661–64, pp. 178–79; Aquinas, *Commentary on the Metaphysics of Aristotle*, Vol. 2., pp. 904–905.

[26] *GP* 1.11, pp. 273–74, and 2.24, p. 326. Again cf. Averroes (ibid.), 1656, p. 175.

This view of astronomy is confusing and has triggered a debate on whether Maimonides was a realist or an instrumentalist about astronomy.[27] If one assumes that epicycles and eccentric orbits are real, questions arise for which there are no ready answers. Given that eccentrics display a different motion than normal spheres, are they composed of a different type of matter? Could a small sphere pass through a larger one? Is there space between eccentric orbits, and if so, what fills it? As Edward Grant indicates, few people ventured opinions on such questions.[28] Surely it would have been safer to avoid questions about the underlying reality of these things and focus on where a particular body will be at a given moment.

But Josef Stern is also right to say that unless there were some interest in the way things are, no one would have been troubled by the lack of agreement between Ptolemy and Aristotle, because Ptolemy's system was more accurate.[29] Whether we are talking about Ptolemy or anyone else, no scientific explanation can save the phenomena at the cost of contradicting a body of accepted results. This is especially true in a system that claims that all of reality proceeds from a single source by virtue of necessity. That is why rather than accept Ptolemy and move on, Maimonides admits perplexity.

To understand Maimonides' view of astronomy, it helps to see what comes directly after his remark about perplexity: a strong statement of the limits of human knowledge (*GP* 2.24, p. 326): "Regarding all that is in the heavens, man grasps nothing but a small measure of what is mathematical; and you know what is in it." Citing Psalms 115:16 ("The heavens are the heavens of the Lord, but

---

[27] For those who think Maimonides adopted some form of instrumentalist, see Pierre Duhem, *To Save the Phenomena: An Essay on the Idea of Physical Theory from Plato to Galileo*, pp. 32–35; Kellner, "On the Status"; Grant, *PSO*, pp. 303–308. For an opposing view, see Langermann, "Perplexity" and "Some Further Reflections."

[28] *PSO*, p. 303.

[29] Josef Stern, "Maimonides on the Growth of Knowledge and Limitations of the Intellect," forthcoming in *Maimonide: Traditions philosophiques et scientifiques médievales arabe, hébraique, latine*, ed. Tony Levy.

the earth hath He given to the sons of man"), he goes on to say that only God knows the nature, substance, motions, and causes of the heavenly bodies and that they are too far away and too high in place or rank for us to agree on assumptions from which conclusions can be drawn. This is in keeping with his claim at *GP* 1.46 that "there is an immense difference between guidance leading to a knowledge of the existence of a thing and an investigation of the true reality of the essence and substance of that thing." The former can be inferred from accidental features or relations, the latter cannot.

Recall that for Aristotle, the proper object of scientific knowledge is that which cannot be otherwise. To see that something cannot be otherwise and know why it cannot, we have to have knowledge of its essence. As Aristotle is fond of saying, we know a thing most fully when we know what it is as opposed to where it is, how big it is, or what qualities it manifests.[30] In view of this, Maimonides' remarks about the distance and rank of the heavenly bodies should be read as saying that essential knowledge in this realm is all but impossible. As we saw, the only thing we have are inferences based on observed motions, which are accidental to the thing in question.

This does not mean that astronomy can never be more than a likely story. At *GP* 2.11 (p. 273), Maimonides admits that some things have been demonstrated, for example, that the orbit of the sun is inclined with respect to the earth. Although this is not subject to doubt, it still does not qualify as a true demonstration, for as Maimonides points out in the next sentence, we do not know what the sphere of the sun is like. Nor did anyone know why it has to be pitched at a certain angle and what purpose that angle serves. At most the demonstration in question would be what Aristotle called a demonstration of the fact (*hoti*) rather than the reasoned fact

---

[30] See, for example, *Metaphysics* 1028a37.

(*dioti*), or, in medieval parlance, a demonstration *quia* rather than a demonstration *propter quid*.[31] The former proceeds from things known from observation (i.e., known to us), and the latter proceed from things known from principles (i.e., known in themselves). Although there is clearly a place for the former, such demonstrations do not give us science in the true sense of the term.

Let us grant that for the period in which Maimonides lived, circular orbits and the inclination of the sun counted as knowledge. Still, they did not provide the astronomer with essential knowledge, and there were areas in which knowledge of any kind had to give way to conjecture. Thus, Maimonides claims there are many cases in which the astronomer can only "suppose as a hypothesis an arrangement (*hay'a*) that renders it possible for the motion of the star to be uniform and circular" (*GP* 1.11, pp. 273–74). The issue, then, is not whether Maimonides is an instrumentalist as modern philosophers of science use the term.[32] When a modern philosopher of science says that electrons, photons, gravitational fields, and ideal gases are explanatory models rather than physical realities, she is speaking from a perspective in which essences, Aristotelian conceptions of demonstration, and realist epistemologies have been abandoned. It is not that scientific theories have failed because they have turned to explanatory models rather than essential forms but that the use of explanatory models is an inevitable feature of trying to make sense of complicated bodies of evidence.

The opposite is true for Maimonides. For him the Aristotelian view of knowledge, truth, and demonstration is correct and sets the standard for anything worthy of being called science. So when

---

[31] Aristotle, *Posterior Analytics* 1.13; cf. *ST* 1.2.2. For the distinction and its application to Maimonides, see Josef Stern, "Maimonides' Demonstrations: Principles and Practice," *Medieval Philosophy and Theology* 10 (2001): 47–84; and "Limitations."

[32] For a similar claim about the astronomy of the sixteenth century, see P. Barker and B. R. Goldstein, "Realism and Instrumentalism in Sixteenth Century Astronomy: A Reappraisal," *Perspectives on Science* 6/3: 232–58.

Maimonides says that astronomy deals with hypotheses that render it possible for the motion of a star to be uniform and circular, he is not making a general claim about scientific knowledge but criticizing astronomy for providing something less. Along these lines, Gad Freudenthal points out that for Maimonides the true perplexity is that although astronomy does not qualify as a proper science in Aristotle's sense of the term, in Ptolemy's case it resembles a proper science by achieving predictive power.[33] As for future progress, the inability of astronomy to explain planetary orbits in a way that preserves Aristotle's understanding of natural motion is not a temporary shortcoming but, in Maimonides' opinion, something that seems to be intractable. In the end we have no choice but to settle for an account of how it is possible to view planetary motion, not a demonstration of why it has to be that way. Without claims of necessity, the ground on which the theory of eternal emanation rests begins to crumble.

IV

Here then is Maimonides' predicament. Although some of his comments are reminiscent of Alghazali (e.g., that no reason can be given for why the stars and planets are attached to their spheres at one point rather than another), the general direction of his argument is that God is not arbitrary and the heavens do exhibit some kind of order. According to *GP* 3.25 (p. 505): "Philosophic speculation similarly requires that there should not be anything futile, frivolous, or vain in all the acts of nature, and all the more in the nature of the spheres, for they are better arranged and ordered because of the nobility of their character." The reference to spheres is telling. Instead of saying that the order and motion of the heavenly

---

[33] Gad Freudenthal, "'Instrumentalism' and 'Realism' as Categories in the History of Astronomy: Duhem vs. Popper, Maimonides vs. Gersonides," *Centaurus* 45 (2003): 96–117.

bodies reflects an arbitrary choice, Maimonides says that it is the last place where we would expect arbitrariness to occur.

This sentiment is also expressed at *GP* 2.19 (p. 310), where he asks how anyone who uses his head could suppose that the positions, measures, and numbers of the stars (and planets) as well as the motions of their various spheres could be fortuitous. Although we do not have a theory that allows us to say why they are ordered this way rather than that, Maimonides is still convinced there is order. His reason cannot be scientific, because he has just argued that there are many things for which science has no explanation. He therefore responds with a theological reason: the heavenly bodies are God's creation, and God acts for a reason even if we are not always in a position to know what it is.

As Maimonides sees it, the idea of divine purpose is undermined by both those who think God chose one from a number of equal alternatives and those who think that the world exists by necessity. The former undermine it because if the alternatives before God are equal, nothing can be accomplished by choosing one over the other. The latter undermine it because if it is impossible for God to produce anything different from what already exists, there is no point in saying that the production of the world was undertaken to realize a purpose. The latter point is made again at *GP* 2.21 (p. 314): "The notions of purpose and particularization only apply to a nonexistent thing for which it is possible to exist just as it was particularized and for which it is also possible not to exist in this fashion."[34] Thus, any evidence for purpose and particularity counts as evidence for creation *de novo*.

Putting Maimonides' objections together, we can say that purpose and particularity involve two factors: choice and a reason for making it. This is why Maimonides resists the idea that the world came about through will or wisdom alone and prefers to say that

---

[34] The same sentiment is expressed at *GP* 3.13, p. 448.

it is the product of both. Against Alghazali, God is not in the position of a thirsty person trying to decide between identical glasses of water. To say that God can will or not will is not to say that God experiences weakness or indecision in making up his mind but that the choice of one alternative over another is not necessary. Against Aristotle, neither is God in the position of overseeing a process he cannot start, stop, or control.

Another way to see this is to consider Maimonides' understanding of necessity. On one occasion, he speaks of natural things including the number and motion of the spheres as being necessary "according to the purpose of one who purposes."[35] As I already mentioned in connection with Leibniz, we can take this to refer to a kind of necessity that does not render its opposite impossible. In other words, the alternatives to the course of action God has chosen are possible but not desirable, so the choice of one over the other is a way of realizing a particular end. This does not mean that we know what God's reasons are for choosing a certain number of spheres and putting them in particular orbits, only that we have grounds for thinking that reasons exist and are not arbitrary.

At *GP* 2.20–21, Maimonides takes up the suggestion that will and purpose might be reconciled with eternity so that behind the procession of the world from God is an exercise of free choice. But, he objects, this is like trying to combine two contraries. A God who cannot do otherwise, and wills what follows from his nature, acts according to necessity no matter how we characterize it. As Maimonides goes on to say, it is like claiming that a person wills to have two hands or two eyes. Because these are normal features of the human body, no decision is required to have them, and no particular purpose is achieved by doing so.

We can understand this better if we return to Avicenna. Finite things are possible in themselves but necessary with respect to their

---

[35] *GP* 2.19, p. 310.

cause.[36] Maimonides' point is that this is too weak. If the world has always existed, it has to exist. Any ascription of purpose or particularity to something that has to exist is illegitimate. What is needed for purpose and particularity is not just possibility but contingency: something that is both possible and possible not. Since only something that came into existence can be possible not, purpose and particularity require creation *do novo.*

## V

Maimonides' strongest argument for particularity is a variation on Alghazali's critique of the "one cause, one effect" principle. According to *GP* 2.22 (p. 317):

> A proposition universally agreed upon, accepted by Aristotle and by all those who have philosophized, reads as follows: It is impossible that anything but a single simple thing should proceed from a simple thing.

A composite thing may have several effects, as when fire softens one thing and dries another. But, as Maimonides points out, the crux of the Aristotelian position is that what first proceeded from God was a single simple intelligence. To this proposition, he adds three others:

(A) There must be a certain conformity between cause and effect. Thus form does not proceed from matter or matter from form.

(B) Every agent acting in virtue of will and purpose accomplishes many different effects.

(C) A whole composed of juxtaposed substances is better described as a composition than a single whole.

---

[36] Again see Avicenna, *Al-Shifā'* 8.7., pp. 366–67. For further discussion of Maimonides' objection, see Seymour Feldman, "The Theory of Eternal Creation in Hasdai Crescas and Some of His Predecessors," *Viator* 2 (1980): 294–95.

I will have more to say on (B) later. For the moment, note that it runs counter to the "one cause, one effect" principle. If an agent acting for a purpose can accomplish many different acts, then it is not limited by rules that govern natural causation.

Maimonides' first claim is that the number of links in the chain of causation is irrelevant. Even if there were a thousand intelligences, the last one would still have to be a single simple thing. He concedes that simplicity can be interpreted loosely. We saw that strict adherence to the "one cause, one effect" principle would require that each intelligence is only aware of itself, because once it has multiple objects of awareness, we have plurality emerging from simplicity. But, Maimonides continues, let us concede that one intelligence can have multiple objects of awareness. The generation of a heavenly sphere from a pure intelligence still violates (A). Rather than solve the problem, the Aristotelians have simply put it off. Insofar as the sphere is complex, its emergence also violates the "one cause, one effect" principle no matter how loosely interpreted.[37]

Nor is that all. Recall that not only is the sphere composed of matter and form, so is the body situated in it. Because the sphere is in motion and transparent while the body is stationary and emits light, it is reasonable to conclude that they are composed of different types of matter. Because they differ both in matter and in form, according to (C) the intelligence that produces them would have to generate four things in addition to the intelligence directly below it. There is also the fact that some of the fixed stars are brighter than others, which implies yet another difference in matter. Each time there is a difference, we get more reason to ask, "Why this rather than that?"

---

[37] For Aquinas' critique of this principle, see *Commentary on the Metaphysics of Aristotle*, Vol. 2., p. 899.

In the earthly realm, matter and form are not united forever: we see material things lose one form and take on a different one all the time. Because all spheres are engaged in circular motion, Maimonides continues, their matter must be the same. If it is the same, why do we not see the transference of form from one sphere to another? One could challenge this by saying that the matter of each sphere is different, but as Maimonides points out, this would mean that their motion is not indicative of their nature and would render the science of astronomy impossible.

Regardless how one conceives of heavenly matter, one must account for the diverse manner in which it appears. This problem was not as acute for Plotinus. In the first place, he restricted the hypostases to intellect and soul and made no attempt to link his theory to the facts of astronomy. In the second place, he provided a framework for saying that the effect can contain features not present in the cause. That is how diversity emerges from unity. But the problem is acute for someone who holds that the diversity visible in the heavens can be understood as a link in a chain where cause and effect must resemble each other.

According to Davidson, the issue at stake is eternal emanation versus a noneternal, voluntary emanation in which God decides to initiate the procession of the world by an act of will.[38] As evidence for this, he cites *GP* 2.12, where Maimonides says that emanation is a fitting metaphor for understanding causation in the metaphysical realm, because it does not involve physical contact. We saw, however, that this chapter is provisional and that Maimonides' approach to emanation is ambivalent.

The question is whether emanation can be combined with free will as easily as Davidson suggests. According to Maimonides, they cannot be combined if the process of emanation has been going

---

[38] *PEC*, pp. 208–209.

on forever. This is why Davidson proposes a noneternal emanation that would allow for a choice on the part of God. The question is, what exactly does this choice amount to? Is it to create the first intelligence and let emanation take over from there or to fine-tune the first intelligence and everything that proceeds from it? If the former, we still have a problem with particularity. If the latter, we still have to explain how a material thing can emerge from a pure intellect.

While Davidson is right to point out that Maimonides objects to eternal emanation on the grounds that it denies free will in God, that is not his only objection. He also objects to the understanding of causality that goes with it. What is gained by saying that the first intelligence comes between God and the outermost sphere? If this world is the product of choice, and God's realm of choice extends to the placement of stars and planets inside spheres, why not say, as Maimonides does at *GP* 2.30, that God created everything at once? Or more fully (*GP* 2.12, p. 281):

> Every existent other than God...was brought into existence by God...and God...existed alone, and nothing else – neither an angel nor a sphere nor what subsists within the sphere [existed with Him]. Afterwards, through His will and His volition, He brought into existence out of nothing all the beings as they are.

This does not deny the existence of angels or intelligences, nor does it deny that they function as a conduit for intelligible forms once everything is on the scene; it simply says that they are the products of a single act by which God confers existence on the created order.

From an Aristotelian perspective, this view is unacceptable because it violates the "one cause, one effect" principle. Because God is one and simple, it is impossible for a multiplicity of effects to follow. Maimonides' response is twofold: (1) there is no reason to suppose that God is limited by this principle, and (2) the Aristotelians themselves do not always adhere to it. As we saw, their account has God produce something triune. Strict adherence to the principle would give us an endless stream of simple intelligences, not a world as we know it.

As for emanation, it is well known that Maimonides employs it to explain prophecy, for which, unlike creation, there is no question of an intellectual being producing a material one.[39] But it is hard to know exactly how he understands it. According to Altmann, the use of "overflow" does not commit him to an actual influx of forms and is nothing but a way of saying that as a result of a variety of factors such as disposition, training, and moral rectitude, the prophet's rational faculty functions in an optimal way.[40] This accords with Maimonides' account of cognition at *GP* 1.68 (pp. 163–65) and 1.73 (p. 209), where there is no mention of an influx of forms.

On the other hand, there are passages where Maimonides refers to the influx of forms in a way that suggests that it is more than just a metaphor.[41] It may be that he himself did not reach a settled position on this issue. Even if he regarded emanation as more than a metaphor, it does not follow that he accepted it as an account of the origin of the world. As we have seen several times, no matter how many intermediaries we posit, the theory of emanation still faces the question of how form gives rise to matter. Because neither Maimonides nor his predecessors want to accept Plotinus' claim that the cause does not resemble its effect, we are left with the claim that a simple, immaterial being is responsible for the existence of the entire finite, complex world that we inhabit. How can this be?

For the answer, we must return to Maimonides' understanding of volition – in particular, the distinction between an act of will and the object willed in the act. We saw that there are two respects

---

[39] See the definition of prophecy at *GP* 2.36, p. 369.
[40] Alexander Altmann, "Maimonides on the Intellect and the Scope of Metaphysics," *Von der mittelalterlichen zur modernen Aufklärung*, p. 83.
[41] See, for example, *GP* 2.4, p. 258; 2.12, p. 278; 3.8, p. 432.

in which this connection differs from normal causation. First, the will can be present and active while the object willed is delayed: I can will now to do something tomorrow. In a causal sequence, the presence of a sufficient cause and the absence of intervening factors imply the presence of the effect. Second, the "one cause, one effect" principle does not apply: the decision to write a book may be simple and take no more than an instant even though the object willed may be complicated and take years to fulfill. This corresponds to Maimonides' principle (B) and indicates that the "one cause, one effect" principle does not apply to acts of will. A third respect, something we have not considered before, is that there is nothing unusual in the claim that an act of will, which is mental, can intend an object that is physical. This happens every time someone chooses to eat or drink.

Taking all this into account, an act of will can produce a diversity beyond the reach of a causal sequence. In causality the nature of the effect is determined by the nature of the cause. Form cannot produce matter or matter form; one thing cannot produce many. In the case of will and object willed, this sort of determination does not apply. God can will anything that is logically possible, including a finite material world. A person could object that if God's will is efficacious, we still have a form of causality. The answer is that we do not have causality as normally understood because there is no passing of an attribute from one thing to another. It is not that the will gives something to the object but that it realizes the object. Again Maimonides' negative theology is critical. Because contingent existence is not a diminished form of necessary existence, there is no resemblance between them.[42] Although we often speak of God's conferring existence on things, Maimonides' point is that this is not like the transference of heat, weight, size, color,

---

[42] *GP* 1.56: "The term 'existent' is predicated of Him . . . and of everything that is other than He, in a purely equivocal sense."

or other natural properties to a recipient. Simply put, existence is a unique property – so unique that the only thing that can confer it is God.

## VI

Maimonides' turn to voluntarism has offended many people. Following Moses Narboni and the Jewish Averroists, Isaac Husik argues that Maimonides forgot the rationalist principles of his own philosophy and took refuge in a doctrine (the will of God) whose only virtue is that no appeal to evidence can refute it.[43] Why abandon science and rationality just because up till now they have not been able to provide a satisfactory explanation of planetary orbits? In Husik's words, Maimonides put in place of science "something else which will always be successful because it will never tell us anything at all and will stifle all investigation."[44] He even went so far as to accuse Maimonides of cowardice.

Although more charitable than Husik, Pines argues in the introduction to his translation of the *Guide* that this objection is substantially correct.[45] It is true that the natural science of Maimonides' day had reached a crisis over the incompatibility of Ptolemy's astronomy with Aristotle's physics. And, says Pines, it is also true that given the difficulty of obtaining knowledge of the heavenly realm, Maimonides' skepticism may have been the only consistent and logical position. However, he continues, "such agnosticism would stultify all that Maimonides set out to accomplish in the *Guide* and would also be quite irreconcilable with his general views, expressed in quite different contexts, on man's highest destination and man's knowledge."[46]

---

[43] Husik, *A History of Medieval Jewish Philosophy*, p. 275.
[44] Ibid., p. 276.
[45] Pines, "Translator's Introduction," p. cxi.
[46] Ibid.

These criticisms miss the mark. By claiming that science reached an impasse from where it has little hope of finding a resolution, Maimonides is not trying to stifle further inquiry. To see this one should keep in mind that revolutions of the sort we associate with Galileo, Newton, or Einstein were unknown in the Middle Ages. So when Maimonides says he doubts anyone will reconcile Ptolemy's predictions with Aristotle's understanding of natural motion, he means that it is hard to imagine a solution that remains within the confines of existing modes of thought. Although there were people who worked on new approaches, it was not until Copernicus, who proposed a theory well beyond anything available to Maimonides and his contemporaries, that an adequate solution became available.[47] Even then it took time before the virtues of the Copernican alternative were apparent. According to Francis Bacon, Copernicus was willing to introduce all sorts of fictions, provided his calculations turned out right.[48]

Beyond that, there is the question of what Maimonides means by purpose. From the fact that God created the world for a purpose, it does not follow that the purpose is in harmony with human wishes and desires. On this issue, Maimonides claims he is in partial agreement with Aristotle.[49] According to Maimonides, it is impossible to inquire after the purpose of something that is eternal, because there is no possibility of its not existing. It follows that if the world

[47] One person who comes to mind is al-Bitruji (1205–74), who argued that all spheres move from east to west, with the fastest movement belonging to the spheres furthest from earth. See al-Bitruji, *On the Principles of Astronomy*, ed. Bernard R. Goldstein. For his influence on Gersonides and Abravanel, see Seymour Feldman, "Abravanel on Maimonides' Critique of the Kalam," *Maimonidean Studies* 1 (1990): 5–25. Although the claim that all spheres move in the same direction may have influenced Copernicus, the claim that the speed of rotation diminishes as one approaches the earth was contradicted by known facts. For criticism of al-Bitruji's theory, see Sabra, "Revolt," pp. 134–38.

[48] For the citation to Bacon and a discussion of the general issue, see Philipp Frank, *Philosophy of Science*, pp. 32–33.

[49] *GP* 3.13, p. 449.

is eternal, there is no point in asking why it exists, why the heavens exist, or why various species exist.[50] One can say that the purpose of an individual is to embody the form of its species and that the first end of the species is to reproduce itself through endless cycles of generation and corruption. But, Maimonides adds, it makes no sense in an Aristotelian framework to ask about the purpose or final end of the species as a whole: why there are whales, elephants, and planets at all.

From the standpoint of human reason, much the same is true in Maimonides' theory. Accordingly, he takes Proverbs 16:4 to mean "the Lord has made everything for his sake," that is, according to his will, and connects it with Genesis 1 ("And God saw that it was good"), as well as 1:31 ("God saw everything he had made, and behold it was very good").[51] It follows that although everything that exists serves a purpose, we have no way of determining what that purpose is other than to say that it conforms to the will and wisdom of God. Why then bring in will at all?

The religious reason is clear: it allows us to take vast portions of sacred literature at its word and to preserve belief in the possibility of miracles.[52] If the world owes its existence to the will of God rather than natural necessity, it is possible that God might make momentary changes in the natural order from time to time. Thus, Maimonides claims (*GP* 1.71, p. 178) that belief in creation *de novo* is common to Judaism, Christianity, and Islam. By contrast, if God does not act for a purpose, it makes no sense to praise God for bringing the world into existence. Still, as we learn at the end of the

---

[50] Maimonides cites a few exceptions in Aristotle's name: plants exist for the sake of animals, and limbs of animals exist for the sake of the whole creature.

[51] In regard to Genesis 1:17–18, where we learn that the stars were created to give light to the earth and rule over day and night, Maimonides argues that this is simply a statement of what their natures are.

[52] For miracles, see *GP* 1.71, p. 178, and 2.25, p. 329. I have more to say on this issue in the next chapter.

Book of Job, God's purpose may be a mystery. Although the world is not chaotic, neither is its purpose and structure transparent. According to Maimonides (*GP* 3.23, p. 496):

> Our intellects do not reach the point of apprehending how these natural things that exist in the world of generation and corruption are produced in time and of conceiving how the existence of the natural force within has originated them. They are not things that resemble what we make.

If this is true of natural phenomena, where direct observation is possible, it is all the more true of heavenly phenomena, where it is not.

The philosophic reason for bringing in will is that it shifts the burden of proof in Maimonides' favor. A defender of eternity has to argue that although there are things in the universe we do not understand at present, in principle we can understand them, and someday we might actually succeed. How do we know this? The only evidence is the record of past successes. Maimonides is willing to accept these successes and to give science its due. What he does not accept is the argument that says, "Because we have had success explaining some things, we have reason to think we will have success explaining all things." As Abravanel points out, scientific anomalies are much more damaging to a defender of eternity than they are to Maimonides because the defender of eternity is committed to a world in which everything happens by necessity.[53]

By contrast, Maimonides is committed to a world in which anomalies or gaps in human understanding are to be expected. Although many of the anomalies that he and his contemporaries puzzled over were later resolved, we should not forget that the advance of science brought to light new anomalies of which they were ignorant. Whatever scientific theory we are dealing with,

---

[53] *Shamayim Ḥadashim (New Heavens)* 1.10–11. For further comment, see Feldman, "Abravanel on Maimonides' Critique," p. 18.

Maimonides' claim comes to this: There are things we cannot explain and reason to think there is some purpose behind them. If there is a purpose, there must be a beginning and a choice of options. Thus, creation *de novo*, although not demonstrated, is the most attractive alternative.

Nothing in this forces Maimonides to give up his belief that intellectual perfection is the highest human achievement. On the contrary, his idea of intellectual perfection includes the warning that one should not deceive oneself into thinking he has a demonstration when he does not and should not pronounce as false something whose contradictory has not been demonstrated.[54] This is why he cannot say for sure that Aristotle is wrong. Because Maimonides thinks Aristotle did not claim to have demonstrated eternity, he continues to hold him in high regard.

[54] *GP* 3.51, p. 619.

# 6

## Nature, Miracles, and the End
## of the World

A NY DISCUSSION OF THE ORIGIN OF THE WORLD RAISES
the question of its end. For Philoponus, and in Jewish tradition Saadia, the two issues are closely linked.[1] According to what
Saadia calls the argument from finitude: (1) the world has a finite
magnitude, (2) what has a finite magnitude can contain only finite power, (3) what contains finite power cannot maintain itself
in existence indefinitely and therefore must have a beginning *and*
end. Therefore, the world was created. As Wolfson notes, Saadia's
argument contains a tacit premise derived from Aristotle: anything
that is perishable must have been generated.[2]

---

[1] Philoponus, *On the Eternity of the World* (ed. Rabe), pp. 230–35; Simplicius, *Commentary on the Physics*, pp. 1330–33; Saadia, *Book of Beliefs and Opinions* 1.1.31, p. 41.

[2] *PK* p. 377. For the reference to Aristotle, see *De Caelo* 281b28.

It is worth noting, as Davidson does, that Saadia's argument differs from that of Philoponus in an important respect.[3] For Saadia, although a finite body cannot maintain *itself* in existence indefinitely, an infinite power can maintain it in existence. So the universe may be created and yet eternal *a parte post*. Philoponus questions this, arguing that it is in the nature of every finite body to lose power over time. Given that the world is inherently destructible and that through infinite time everything that is possible will come to pass, it seems that a finite body cannot last forever even if it is maintained by an infinite one.[4]

Although Maimonides does not use a version of this argument to establish creation, we have seen that he accepts the claim that anything that is generated will pass away.[5] As long as this principle holds, any argument for the creation of the world *de novo* will entail its eventual destruction. If Maimonides accepted the Platonic theory of creation, this would pose no problem because he takes that theory to hold that eventually the heavens will perish. We saw, however, that he does not accept it.[6] In fact, he devotes three chapters (*GP* 2.27–29) to showing that once created, the world will last forever. In so doing, he follows Augustine, who rejects the suggestion that only something that has no beginning can last forever; in short, that eternity *a parte post* presupposes eternity *a parte ante*.[7] Although creation *de novo* is a foundation of the Law, in Maimonides' opinion, belief in its eventual destruction is not.

---

[3] *PEC*, pp. 89–92, 102.

[4] On the principle that what is destructible will eventually be destroyed, see *De Caelo* 283a 24–25. Cf. *GP* 2.1, p. 247: "Now it is indubitable . . . that what is possible in regard to a species must necessarily come about."

[5] *GP* 2.27, p. 332.

[6] The difference between the Mosaic and Platonic views on the eventual destruction of the world requires me to part company with Samuelson, "Maimonides' Doctrine," pp. 258 ff.

[7] Augustine, *City of God* 10.31.

Apart from Maimonides' opinion, the destruction of the world raises troubling questions. If the world is going to be destroyed, why did God create it in the first place? What happens to the belief that God is a faithful and steadfast ruler? What happens to claims of eternal life or promises of salvation? In view of these questions, it should come as no surprise that Maimonides thinks the sacred literature of Judaism is committed to the eternity of the world *a parte post*. The question is why, if the world was created, will it continue to exist; in fact, not only will it continue to exist, but in Maimonides' view, it will continue in its present form.

The immediate answer is given by Maimonides himself at *GP* 2.27. Although it is true that anything generated *by a natural process* will pass away, he has argued that creation is not a natural process, for unlike the generation of a plant from a seed, the creation of the world does not involve the transition from potency to act and thus does not require a material cause. Accordingly, *GP* 2.17, p. 332:

> For we do not assert that it [the world] has been generated according to the rule applying to the generation of the natural things that follow a natural order. For what is generated in accordance with the course of nature must of necessity pass away in accordance with nature.

In place of natural generation, Maimonides has the will of God. Because there is no resemblance between the two, there is no reason to think that the destruction of natural things in the world implies the destruction of the world as a whole. To repeat: creation is unique.

Once this is granted, Maimonides can deny eternity *a parte ante* but affirm it *a parte post*. If, as some believe, he is secretly committed to the former, there would be no reason for him to devote three chapters to a defense of the latter because it would follow immediately. What has always existed must exist and thus cannot be subject to destruction. In short, the end of the world is an issue worth discussing only if creation *de novo* is granted. Because Maimonides rejects the Platonic view of creation, we have no choice but to understand creation as both *de novo* and *ex nihilo*, exactly the view he said he was going to defend back at *GP* 2.13.

I

We can begin by recognizing that for Maimonides the world is not the only thing that will last forever; so will the throne of glory, the souls of the righteous, the heavens, the earth, the laws governing them, and many of the things contained within.[8] Without going into a detailed discussion of these things, we can see that Maimonides' list is quite general: while some of the things on it are immaterial, some are not. What he seems to be saying is that the cosmic order is permanent, so that having created it, God will keep it going. At *GP* 2.28, he cites Psalms 104:5 ("Who did establish the earth on its foundations, That it should not be moved forever and ever") and points out that the phrase "forever and ever" (*le-olam va-ed*) is stronger than "forever" (*le-olam*) alone, as Solomon uses it at Ecclesiastes 1:4 ("The earth will abide forever"). In conjunction with Exodus 15:18 ("The Lord shall reign forever and ever"), Maimonides takes the stronger expression to imply the eternity of the world *a parte post*.

His view is strengthened by citing Psalms 148:1–6, where the angels, the hosts of heaven, the sun and moon, the stars, and the waters above the heavens are asked to praise God because "he commanded, and they were created. He has established them for ever and ever." Although the next few verses do not mention the phrase "forever and ever," they go on to include sea monsters, fire,

---

[8] For further discussion of this point, see Roslyn Weiss, "Maimonides on the End of the World," *Maimonidean Studies* 3 (1992–93): 195–218.

hail, snow, wind, mountains, trees, even creeping things and winged fowl. The reference to divine command suggests free will rather than natural causation. God brought these things into existence and saw to it that they would exist for all time. This coincides with Maimonides' rejection of natural causation as stated in *GP* 2.27:

> Rather does the matter [whether something exits or not] inevitably depend on His will: if He wills, He causes the thing to pass away; and if He wills, He causes it to last; or it depends on what is required by His wisdom.

As we saw, Maimonides often uses *will* and *wisdom* as near synonyms, implying that the former is not capricious and does nothing in vain.

The issue becomes more complicated when Maimonides returns to Ecclesiastes 3:14 ("I know that whatever God does shall last forever; nothing can be added to it, nor anything taken away from it"). If the creator is perfect, how could it happen that his creation begins to unravel? Commenting on this passage, Maimonides adds (*GP* 2.28, p. 335):

> Now the works of the deity are most perfect, and with regard to them there is no possibility of an excess or a deficiency. Accordingly, they are of necessity permanently established as they are, for there is no possibility of something calling for a change in them.

As he goes on to argue, the view of Solomon as expressed in Ecclesiastes is consistent with Deuteronomy 32:4 ("The Rock, his work is perfect") and implies that all of God's creations are perfect, as required by divine wisdom.

Maimonides' interpretation of Ecclesiastes can be seen as an extension of his view of the Messiah as found in the *Mishneh Torah*. The days of the Messiah will be marked by an end to war, strife, and famine and produce an environment in which people can devote their energies to science and eventually to worship of God. But against the background of centuries of speculation about how life will be lived when the Messiah comes, Maimonides claims that at a deeper level, things will go on as before. There will still be rich and poor, strong and weak. There will still be the normal cycle of birth, growth, and death – even for the Messiah. In Maimonides' words: "Let no one think that in the days of the Messiah any of the laws of nature will be set aside, or any innovation be introduced into creation. The world will follow its normal course."[9] Because the world will follow its normal course, the Torah will still be valid. In fact, the restoration of sovereignty to Israel will allow it to fulfill all the commandments, including those dealing with the sacrificial cult.

All of this raises a crucial question: Is the eternity of the world *a parte post* due to the fact that God keeps it in existence or that it is inherently indestructible? In the recent literature, Seymour Feldman opts for the first alternative, arguing that, left to its own devices, the world would exhaust its power and cease to be. Because God does not want this to happen, he maintains the world *contra naturam*.[10] Along these lines, Feldman sees a parallel between Maimonides' position and *Timaeus* 41a–b, where the Demiurge says he could destroy the created gods but chooses not to. Roslyn Weiss opts for the second alternative. Because creation is a miracle, and the product of creation has no deficiency, the only thing that could destroy the world is another miracle.[11] Recall that in responding to Aristotle's second argument for eternity derived from the nature of the world, Maimonides argues that Aristotle was right to think that prime matter is not subject to generation and destruction if

---

[9] *Mishneh Torah* 14, Kings and Wars, 12.1; cf. *Perek Helek.*
[10] Seymour Feldman, "The End of the Universe in Medieval Jewish Philosophy," *AJS Review* 11 (1986): 53–77.
[11] Weiss, "Maimonides."

that means that it is generated in the way that individual things are. Rather, it is created *ex nihilo* without intermediaries. But he adds: "Its Creator may, if He wishes to do so, render it entirely and absolutely nonexistent" (*GP* 2.17, p. 297).

The mention of cataclysmic events and action *contra naturam* raises the question of Maimonides' attitude toward miracles. Given his belief that the world will follow its normal course, we would expect a fair amount of skepticism. It is well known that he regards much of prophetic experience as a dream or vision rather than the receipt of veridical sense data. Along these lines, Abraham's hospitality to the three visitors, Jacob's wrestling with the angels, and Balaam's speaking to his donkey are interpreted as visions rather than reports of actual events.[12] In fact, Maimonides is so convinced of this that he claims we should assume dreams or visions are involved even when the text does not explicitly say so. In regard to Moses' encounter with God on the mountaintop, Maimonides argues (*GP* 1.21, pp. 50–51) that one can believe *either* that the whole episode was an intellectual apprehension involving no recourse to the senses *or* that the vision of a created object is implied, but there is little question that he prefers the former. In regard to the future, he warns people not to rely on divine intervention to rescue a desperate situation. Rather, progress will come by natural means, so people will have to rely on the development of their own talents.[13] Even the granting of eternal life is not a miracle

---

[12] *GP* 2.42. Also see *GP* 2.36, pp. 368–69, where he questions whether the sun really stood still for Joshua at Gibeon.

[13] For further discussion of this point, see Aviezer Ravitzky, "'To the Utmost Human Capacity': Maimonides on the Days of the Messiah," in *PM*, pp. 221–56; and Menachem Kellner, *Maimonides on "The Decline of the Generations" and the Nature of Rabbinic Authority*, p. 75. It is true that Maimonides takes a less skeptical view of miracles in the "Epistle to the Jews of Yemen" and emphasizes the saving grace of God. But I agree with David Hartman (*Crisis and Leadership: Epistles of Maimonides*, p. 151) that we have to consider the context in which he wrote it. Rather than a philosophic treatise, it is a letter written for the purpose of strengthening a community in a time of crisis.

but the passage of the acquired intellect into a purely intellectual realm.[14]

We saw, however, that one of Maimonides' criticisms of Aristotle is that if no volition can arise in God, God would be incapable of doing anything new and could not change the shape of a fly's wing. We also saw that one of the advantages of creation *de novo* is that it allows us to preserve belief in the possibility of miracles. The key word is *possibility*. Again Maimonides wants us to see that God is not limited by natural causation.[15] If he were, the world would be eternal *a parte ante* and *a parte post*. So it is possible for God to accomplish something that nature alone cannot. Once we admit this, particular miracles must be approached on a case-by-case basis. If there is good reason to accept one, we should; if not, no religious principle is violated by seeking another explanation. Although he does not want people to rely on miracles, Maimonides argues that we should approach some of them, especially those produced by Moses, with an open mind. How does he reconcile this with the claim that the world will follow its normal course?

In *Eight Chapters* (8), he accepts the rabbinic view according to which all miracles were provided for during the first six days of creation.[16] The idea is that God inserted into the nature of the sea that it would divide when the Israelites crossed and into the nature of the sun that it would stand still for Joshua. This enables him to reconcile belief in the possibility of miracles with the rabbinic dictum "The world goes its customary way."[17] Commenting on Ecclesiastes 1:9 ("What was is what will be; what has been done is what will be done; there is nothing new under the sun"), Maimonides claims: "When

[14] See *GP* 3.54, p. 635, where Maimonides claims that intellectual perfection gives an individual "permanent perdurance." This doctrine is spelled out in greater detail in *MT* 1, Laws of Repentance, 8.3.

[15] Keep in mind, however, that according to *GP* 3.15, God is limited by the laws of logic.

[16] *Genesis Rabbah* 5.4; *Kohelet Rabbah* 1.3.

[17] *Avodah Zarah* 54b.

it [a miracle] takes place at the time it was supposed to, something new is presumed to occur, but that is not so."[18] All that is happening is that the thing in question is adhering to the nature with which God originally endowed it. Although the course of history may make it seem as if God wills things serially and the natures of things change from time to time, everything was set during creation.

This seems like a makeshift solution. To say that it was in the nature of the sea to divide at one point is to ascribe to it a peculiar property unlike anything science can detect. Once we do this, the claim that the world goes its customary way is hollow. After all, a sea that divides is hardly a customary phenomenon. By the time he gets to the *Guide*, however, Maimonides modifies his position.[19] Although he cites the rabbinic view at *GP* 2.29 and does not openly criticize it, neither does he say that he accepts it. On one hand, he wants to retain the view that God does not will things serially. This is in keeping with the distinction between willing change and changing one's will. If all miracles were provided for during creation, God does not have to make a new decision every time divine incursion is required. Rather, there is one decision that holds for all time. On the other hand, he wants to abandon the idea of an essential nature that contains unpredictable qualities.

Accordingly, he argues (*GP* 2.29, p. 345) that if a miracle occurs, it is only a temporary change in the way things behave and leaves their customary natures intact:

> I have said that a thing does not change its nature in such a way that the change is permanent merely in order to be cautious

---

[18] *Eight Chapters* 8.

[19] For further discussion of the shift in Maimonides' position, see Hannah Kasher, "Biblical Miracles and the Universality of Natural Laws: Maimonides' Three Methods of Harmonization," *Journal of Jewish Thought and Philosophy* 8 (1998): 25–52. According to Kasher, part of the reason for the shift is that in *Eight Chapters*, Maimonides wants to reject the view of the Mutakallimūn according to which God wills something different in each moment of time, while in the *Guide*, he wants to reject the view of Aristotle, according to which God cannot will anything new.

with regard to the miracles. For although the rod was turned into a serpent, the water into blood, and the pure and noble hand became white without a natural cause that necessitated this, these and similar things were not permanent and did not become another nature.

According to this view, it is not part of the nature of a rod to turn into a serpent. When Moses performed the miracle, a genuine anomaly occurred. Because the anomaly was short-lived, the nature of the rod is exactly as described by natural science. All of this presupposes that a miracle cannot go on forever. If it did, two things would follow: (1) what was once viewed as an anomaly would now be seen as a customary occurrence, forcing us to revise our conception of the original nature; (2) people would begin to take the miracle for granted, so it would no longer command attention.[20] In regard to (2), Maimonides cites Ecclesiastes 3.14 again: "And God has made it so, that they should fear before Him."[21]

In assessing Maimonides' position, we should keep in mind that ancient and medieval science did not have a Newtonian conception of natural law. The world that science investigates is a composite of matter and form. Because matter is unruly and occasionally refuses to accept form, it is not surprising that anomalies occur. Along these lines, Aristotle distinguishes the exactness demanded by the mathematician from that demanded by the natural philosopher on the grounds that the former applies only to immaterial things.[22] In this scheme, a natural law is a generalization that holds "always or for the most part" and can admit exceptions without being overturned.[23]

---

[20] *GP* 3.50, p. 616: "It is well known that it is impossible and inconceivable that a miracle lasts permanently throughout the succession of generations so that all men may see it."

[21] *GP* 2.28, pp. 335–36.

[22] Aristotle, *Metaphysics* 995a15–20.

[23] Aristotle, *Physics* 196b10–15. Cf. *GP* 2.20, p. 312.

It is therefore misleading to say that according to Maimonides miracles *violate* nature. Because science demands generality, exceptions lie outside its domain. To use a modern term, Aristotelian science takes no account of singularities. This is why Maimonides insists that however much attention they grab, miracles leave the natural order intact. Seen in this light, miracles pose a different problem than that posed by planetary orbits. In one case, we have recurring phenomena that science cannot explain; in the other, temporary ones. If the former represents a failure of science, the latter represents nothing more than an occasional limitation.

The difference between Maimonides and Aristotle is that the latter thought exceptions to natural laws were the result of chance, whereas the former sees miracles as the result of design. It is not by chance that the rod turned into a serpent but because God willed it. Although the laws of nature may still be intact, Maimonides allows for the possibility that God can do something extraordinary. At *GP* 2.29 (p. 346), he sums up his position as follows:

> We agree with Aristotle with regard to one half of his opinion and we believe that what exists is eternal *a parte ante* and will last forever with that nature which He . . . has willed; that nothing in it will be changed in any respect unless it be in some particular of it miraculously – although He . . . has the power to change the whole of it, or to annihilate it, or to annihilate any nature in it that He wills. However, that which exists has had a beginning, and at first nothing at all existed except God. His wisdom required that He should bring creation into existence at the time when He did do it, and that what He has brought into existence should not be annihilated nor any of its natures changed except in certain particulars that He willed to change.

The fact that God has the power to change or annihilate the natural order implies that it is neither necessary in itself nor necessary with respect to its cause. As we have seen, its existence follows from a free choice. This is why belief in the possibility of miracles and creation *de novo* go hand in hand. Because the natural order is not necessary, extraordinary events can occur when God deems it appropriate.

## II

Let us return to the question of eternity *a parte post*. To paraphrase Weiss: Is it the destruction of the world or its preservation that requires a show of God's power?[24] In one respect, it is the destruction. If the world follows its normal course, it will exist forever with the qualities God has given it. Because the only thing that can alter this is an act of annihilation, whose possibility is granted but whose likelihood rejected, preservation of the world is the only reasonable conclusion.

The question is: how is it preserved? Did God give the world a quality that allows it to exist on its own, or does the world need God to keep going? The crux of Maimonides' position is that the origin of the world is not the result of a natural process but of an act of will. If this is true, it is only by an act of will that it is still here. In this respect, Feldman is right. The danger in emphasizing will is that it encourages us to think of God as a mechanic who keeps an old car running long after it is ready for the junkyard. This is clearly wrong. The world's eternity *a parte post* is part of God's original plan and does not require daily decisions about what to do. Although God has the power to destroy the world, we have seen that that applies in principle only. Again from Ecclesiastes 3.14 (cited by Maimonides at *GP* 2.28, p. 335): "Whatever God does shall last forever."

So the world is indestructible. But the reason for this is not, as Weiss suggests, that it has an *inherent* capacity to keep itself going.[25]

---

[24] Weiss, "Maimonides," p. 209.
[25] Weiss, "Maimonides," pp. 207, 209.

Like Philoponus, Saadia, or Aristotle, Maimonides subscribes to the principle that what has a finite magnitude can only contain finite power.[26] In fact, this principle plays an important role in his proof for the existence of God. From it Maimonides concludes that the power that resides in a heavenly sphere is insufficient to move it for an infinite amount of time.[27] I take this to mean that no natural reason can be found to explain the world's eternity *a parte post*. As with creation, we have no choice but to invoke the will of God.

At this point, it is important to keep in mind what Maimonides does not say. Recall that the heavens, the throne of glory, and the souls of the righteous will exist forever. Maimonides could have said that the reason for this is that their natures make them immune from natural processes involving corruption or decay. The fact is, however, that he gives a very different reason: again, the will of God (*GP* 2.27, pp. 332–33). Because existence is not necessary to these things and must be given to them by the will of God, the only reason that can be cited for their continued existence is that same will.

This is not the first time Maimonides makes this point. According to *GP* 1.69, not only can no reason be found to explain the eternity of the world *a parte post*, likewise no reason can be found to explain its existence for one second without God's help. The point of that chapter is that the relation between God and the world is not analogous to that between a sculptor and her creation. It is not that by destroying the world God would be interfering with something that is capable of existing on its own. A better analogy would be that between the heart and the rest of the body. Once the cause is removed, the effect vanishes immediately. If this is true, it makes no difference whether we are talking about the origin of the world, its existence at this moment, or its existence a billion years from

[26] *MT* 1, Basic Principles, 1.7; *GP* 2, Introduction, p. 237. Cf. Aristotle, *Physics* 266b25–26.
[27] *GP* 2.1, p. 244.

now; according to Maimonides, the only reason that can be given for its existence at any point is the will of God.

As I indicated earlier, *GP* 1.69 is a provisional chapter, the meaning of which is clouded by the issue of emanation. But the claim that the world needs God in every moment of its history comes up again at *GP* 1.72. Just as there is a force that connects the parts of the body, governs them, and safeguards their well-being, so, Maimonides argues, there is something that sets the world into motion, rules it, and protects it from harm. In the former case, the force involved is nature; in the latter case, God. Because *GP* 1.72 does not deal with creation per se, I take it that the dependence of the world on God would be admitted by all hands. For the historical Aristotle, God thinks and by so doing gives the heavenly bodies a reason to stay in motion. For Alfarabi and Avicenna, God thinks and causes the procession of the first intelligence. For Maimonides, God's thought is not enough: the evidence of particularity shows that we also need God's will. Once the relevance of will is granted, it is no longer possible to explain the existence of the world by natural causes alone. If the will of God is a factor in the creation of the world, it must also be a factor in the governance and protection of the world.

In defense of a naturalistic reading, Weiss directs us to Maimonides' remarks at *GP* 2.28 (cited earlier) – in particular, the claim that the works of God are of necessity permanently established. There is no reason to think that the necessity mentioned here is natural, however. On the contrary, we saw that Maimonides argues the kind of necessity involved in creation is that which follows "according to the purpose of one who purposes." Again from *GP* 2.29: "What exists is eternal *a parte post* and will last forever with that nature which He . . . has willed." Abstracting from that will and looking at the world on its own terms, neither a first moment nor eternity *a parte post* are possible. Rather than a quality found *in* the world, existence is something God confers *upon* it. This is what enables Maimonides to say that creation is an act of graciousness, because God gives existence to something that has no ability to give it to itself and no right to claim it on its own.

III

As usual, Maimonides is reluctant to claim too much for what he has argued. From the fact that God wills an orderly world that lasts forever, it does not follow that we can understand everything that order contains. Note, for example, that after citing Deuteronomy 32:4 at *GP* 2.28, Maimonides cites it again at *GP* 3.49 (pp. 605–606). This time it is not the permanence of the world to which he calls attention but its relative opacity:

> It says that just as the things made by Him are consummately perfect, so are His commandments consummately just. However, our intellects are incapable of apprehending the perfection of everything that He has made and the justice of everything He has commanded. We only apprehend the justice of some of His commandments just as we only apprehend some of the marvels in the things He has made, in the parts of the body of animals and in the motions of the spheres. What is hidden from us in both these classes of things is much more considerable than what is manifest.

These remarks are prompted by the second part of the verse, which reads: "For all His ways are judgment."

The claim that natural causes are insufficient to account for every feature of the world reraises the question of Maimonides' attitude to science. To see what is wrong with the suggestion that his philosophy undermines scientific inquiry, let us return to the previous citation. According to Maimonides, our intellects are incapable of apprehending the justice of everything God commanded. This did not prevent him, however, from writing fourteen volumes of the *Mishneh Torah* to explain that part of the Law whose justice we can understand. Nor did it prevent him from saying that it is our duty to study the Law so as to understand it to the best of our ability. By the same token, we cannot apprehend the perfection of everything God has done. But this does not prevent physics and astronomy from explaining whole bodies of information or Maimonides from saying that we are obliged to study them as well. We saw that once he gets beyond the opening sentence of Genesis and explicates the activities of the first six days of creation, he is perfectly happy to rely on Aristotelian physics.

The Mutakallimūn denied the existence of essential natures and argued that every assignment of color, taste, smell, humanity, sensation, or rationality to things is arbitrary. In this world, everything is a miracle. In Maimonides' world things have essential natures that are given to them by God. Although God could change the natures of things at any moment, doing so would make scientific study of the world impossible and contradict the original intention God had in creating it. The danger in speaking of a will guided by wisdom is that people will think will is nothing but wisdom. In this connection, Weiss remarks that the link between will and wisdom provides the strongest support for those who think that Maimonides is committed to the eternity of the world *a parte ante*.[28] Because Maimonides often characterizes God's wisdom as "perpetual and immutable," it might seem as if God's will should be perpetual and immutable as well. If that is the case, the past history of the world would be symmetrical with its future history in the sense that both extend to infinity.

---

[28] Weiss, "Maimonides," pp. 211–12, n. 41. According to Weiss, the line between a will bound by perpetual and immutable wisdom on one hand and necessity on the other is perilously fine. As she points out, this claim is supported by *GP* 2.18, p. 301: "For, in our opinion, volition too is consequent upon wisdom; all these being one and the same," as well as similar passages. Recall, however, that Maimonides resists any attempt to combine will and purpose with necessity and maintains that such a view would be like combining two contraries.

So stated, this objection is a version of Aristotle's third argument for eternity derived from the nature of God. According to that argument, the world is the product of divine wisdom. Because that wisdom is eternal and unchanging, the world must be eternal and unchanging as well. We saw, however, that Maimonides objects to this argument on the grounds that it presupposes knowledge beyond the reach of the human intellect, because we are ignorant of the rule of divine wisdom and the decision made by it. I take this to mean that Maimonides did not think the identity of will and wisdom in God is a sufficient reason for affirming eternity *a parte ante*. On what grounds can we show that God's wisdom can only consider logical necessity and has no acquaintance with the kind of knowledge involved in choosing the best of several alternatives? In view of this, it is hardly surprising that Maimonides claims (*GP* 2.23, p. 321) that Aristotle's position involves "a presumptuous assertion with regard to the deity," a sentiment that is repeated when he summarizes his position at *GP* 2.29 (p. 346).

To defend eternity *a parte ante*, a person would have to do more than defend the unity of will and wisdom in God, because Maimonides' position is that our understanding of God is so meager that it is compatible with either the Mosaic, Platonic, or Aristotelian positions. That is why none of these alternatives is demonstrable. Rather, to defend eternity *a parte ante*, a person would have to show that the evidence Maimonides presents on behalf of particularity can be explained by causal necessity; that is, a defender of eternity would have to give an account of the origin, identity, and motion of the heavenly bodies that renders any alternative implausible, if not impossible. In view of the fact that we do not know the natures of these things, it is hard to see how this task could be fulfilled.

In the end, eternity *a parte ante* remains a possibility but one that saddles its proponents with a heavy burden and plays havoc with the Torah. By contrast, eternity *a parte post* places no such burden on its proponents and allows Maimonides to claim support from the Book of Ecclesiastes. There are, of course, prophetic passages that describe cataclysmic events that shake heaven and earth to their foundations, but Maimonides has little trouble showing that these passage are hyperbolic descriptions of the collapse of a mighty kingdom.

With his usual respect for Aristotle, Maimonides claims partial agreement with his opinion. Once God confers existence on the world, the course of nature is and will always be as Aristotle described it. The only exceptions to this claim are (1) the places where, as Aristotle himself came to see, his astronomy breaks down and (2) the fact that having been created, the world will not pass away. Neither of these undermines the legitimacy of science as Maimonides conceives it. The first calls attention to the precarious position in which medieval astronomy found itself; the second repeats the familiar claim that the existence and duration of the world are not analogous to the generation and destruction of a natural object within it. Although it is true that the initial act of creation is outside the scope of scientific inquiry, Maimonides never hesitates to say that it was undertaken for a purpose that is in large part to construct an orderly and stable universe.

Simply put: to argue that science has limits is not to undermine it. In the Parable of the Palace, the study of natural science is a prerequisite for entry into the inner court. But the study of natural science has two aspects. One is to acquaint us with the ways or works of God so that we will come to love God; the other is to allow us to see that the categories that apply in natural science do not apply to God. In connection with the latter, Maimonides points out that a person may have to labor in a science for many years to get to the point where this becomes clear.[29] Although the first function may induce love of God, it cannot provide a conceptual framework in

[29] *GP* 1.59, p. 138.

which to comprehend God or the heavenly realm. Thus (*GP* 2.22, pp. 319–20):

> Everything that Aristotle has said about all that exists from beneath the sphere of the moon to the center of the earth is indubitably correct.... On the other hand, everything that Aristotle expounds with regard to the sphere of the moon and that which is above it is, except for certain things, something analogous to guessing and conjecturing. All the more does this apply to what he says about the order of the intellects and to some of the opinions regarding the divine that he believes; for the latter contain grave incongruities and perversities that... he cannot demonstrate.

I take the reference to "certain things" that Aristotle got right to refer to the claim that God exists and is neither a body nor a force in a body. Beyond that, Maimonides' view is that natural science does not live up to the standards of proof that Aristotle himself established for it.

In regard to creation, this means that natural science is incapable of demonstrating the eternity of the world *a parte ante* or refuting its eternity *a parte post*. In both cases, Maimonides' arguments leave open the possibility that the opposite is true. If the scale were evenly balanced between Maimonides and Aristotle, scriptural evidence would tip it in Maimonides' direction. The fact is, however, that Maimonides' critique of natural science is designed to show that the scales are not evenly balanced, so that apart from religious considerations, philosophic argument supports belief in a created world that will endure forever.


IV

As I indicated earlier, the focal point of Maimonides' discussion of the end of the world is the rejection of the Platonic account of creation. Both the Platonic and the Aristotelian accounts reject the creation of everything *ex nihilo*. If Aristotle's naturalism rejects creation *de novo*, on Maimonides' reading, Plato's rejects eternity *a parte post*. The reason Maimonides spends more time on Aristotle is that creation *de novo* is a foundation of the Law, whereas neither its destruction nor its eternity *a parte post* is. Although eternity *a parte post* is implied by a number of biblical and rabbinic sources, Maimonides does not accord it the same status as creation.

Despite these differences, his critique of the Platonic and Aristotelian alternatives follows the same pattern: naturalistic explanations fail when we approach the extremities of existence. The reason for this is that naturalism is based on sense experience, which by definition tells us the way things are now. Thus, any extrapolation from sense experience to the way they were at the point of origin or will be at the end point is questionable. Note, for example, that despite their adherence to naturalism, the Platonic and Aristotelian alternatives arrive at opposite opinions in regard to the beginning and end of the world. Not only are these opinions not compelling, according to Maimonides they fly in the face of the prophetic tradition as he understands it.

Reference to the prophetic tradition is important because Maimonides thinks that the opinions one holds on prophecy are similar to the ones one holds on creation (*GP* 2.32, p. 360). Unfortunately, his remarks on this topic are ambiguous and have long troubled commentators:

> The opinions of people concerning prophecy are like their opinions concerning the eternity of the world or its creation in time. I mean by this that just as the people to whose mind the existence of the deity is firmly established, have, as we have set forth, three opinions concerning the eternity of the world or its creation in time, so are there also three opinions concerning prophecy.

As with creation, Maimonides examines a variety of opinions and asks which is the strongest. Unlike his proofs for the existence of

God, there is no attempt to reason from premises to conclusion. For my purposes, the question is whether there is anything in common between the opinions on creation and the opinions on prophecy other than the number three.

The first opinion on prophecy is that of the multitude of those among the pagans who accept prophecy and also some of those who profess the Law: God can turn anyone he wishes into a prophet. In effect, prophecy is a miracle. The second is that of the philosophers: prophecy is a perfection of human nature for which appropriate training is necessary. On this view, it is impossible that an ignoramus can become a prophet or that an individual who is suited to be prophet does not achieve it. Thus, prophecy is a natural phenomenon. The third is "the opinion of our Law and the foundation of our doctrine." According to Maimonides, it is identical with the philosophic view except for one thing: although God cannot turn an ignoramus into a prophet, he can prevent someone from becoming a prophet who is otherwise suited for it. In this way, intellectual perfection is a necessary rather than a sufficient condition for being a prophet. After receiving the necessary training, an individual must hope that God does not interfere.

For both creation and prophecy one opinion represents a naturalistic alternative and one the foundation of the Law. But there are also differences. All the opinions on creation are held by people with reputations for intellectual proficiency; none is attributed to the multitude. One position on prophecy is presented as a qualification of another, whereas each position on creation stands by itself. Let us refer to the various opinions as $C_1$, $C_2$, and $C_3$ and $P_1$, $P_2$, and $P_3$. Although Maimonides' explicit remarks leave no doubt that he prefers $C_1$ and $P_3$, it is not clear how these positions relate to one another. There is also the question of whether his explicit remarks are meant to hide a preference for something else.

We can begin by looking at $P_3$. There is a tradition that sees $P_3$ as a synthesis of $P_1$ and $P_2$, but Lawrence Kaplan is right in saying that this view is untenable for two reasons: (1) if there were something in P1 worth preserving, it is unlikely that Maimonides would criticize it as harshly as he does; and (2) Maimonides explicitly says that P3 is like P2, the difference being that according to P3 prophecy can be withheld.[30] Citing the views of several medieval commentators as precedent, Kaplan argues that considered in itself, prophecy is a natural phenomenon that does not require divine intervention. The only place where divine intervention is involved is when God decides to deny prophecy, as in the case of Baruch.[31] Thus, Maimonides compares P3 to God's preventing Jeroboam from moving his arm or the King of Aram's army from seeing.[32] Because moving an arm and seeing are natural phenomena, it is God's interference with them that constitutes a miracle.

It could be objected that because God can always prevent someone from being a prophet, God must make a decision *not* to interfere with prophecy if nature is to take its normal course, so that the will of God is needed whether a person becomes a prophet or not. This is right in the sense that nothing can happen without the will of God. The point is, however, that a decision not to interfere is not miraculous. To work a miracle, God must bring about something different from what nature would do left to its own devices even though God is responsible for the existence of nature in the first place.

Still, P3 is problematic. As several of Maimonides' medieval commentators (chiefly Abravanel, Efodi, and Shem Tov) recognized,

---

[30] Lawrence Kaplan, "Maimonides on the Miraculous Element in Prophecy," *Harvard Theological Review* 70 (1977): 233–56. For criticism of Kaplan and the articles by Davidson and Harvey discussed later, see Samuelson, "Maimonides' Doctrine," pp. 261–71. For a more recent discussion, which concludes with a naturalistic theory of prophecy and an Aristotelian theory of creation, see Howard Kreisel, *Prophecy: The History of an Idea in Medieval Jewish Philosophy*, pp. 222–30.

[31] Jeremiah 45:3. See *GP* 2.32, p. 362. Note, however, that after saying that God denied prophecy to Baruch, Maimonides goes on to suggest that there may be a naturalistic explanation: prophecy was too great for him.

[32] *GP* 2.32, pp. 361–62.

P3 commits Maimonides to the view that God might intervene to prevent someone from obtaining a perfection he has trained for and to which he would ordinarily be suited. How can a benevolent God do this? Does God not want every person to reach the highest possible state of perfection? Does Maimonides himself not cite (*GP* 3.17, p. 470) the rabbinic dictum according to which God does not withhold from any creature what it deserves? Moreover, Maimonides says (*GP* 2.32, p. 362) that he has already explained in the *Commentary on the Mishnah* and the *Mishneh Torah* that prophecy requires adequate training. There is no reference in either work to the denial of prophecy. On what basis then could Maimonides accept P3?

Kaplan responds by pointing out that Maimonides is in fundamental agreement with the philosophers. When prophecy occurs it is a natural phenomenon. But above and beyond any natural phenomenon is the will of God and the possibility of miracles. Just as the miraculous withholding of sight is not part of an ordinary theory of vision, so the miraculous withholding of prophecy is not part of Maimonides' ordinary theory of prophecy. Nonetheless it is still true that God can withhold natural perfections from a creature to accomplish a greater end. Do we have evidence that this has happened? Kaplan answers that the issue is not whether it *has* happened but whether in principle it could. As we saw in the previous section, it is the possibility of miracles that interests Maimonides, not reports of this or that occurrence. Once the possibility is granted, it follows that while nature can follow its normal course and usually does, extraordinary events are possible.

Accordingly Kaplan suggests that P1 corresponds to C2, P3 to C1, and P2 to C3. His reasoning is as follows. P2 (the opinion of the philosophers) and C3 (Aristotle) represent unqualified naturalism. P3 and C1 both accept the possibility of miracles and are identified as the opinion of the Law. As for P1 and C2, the Platonic theory of creation has God create whatever he wants out of formless matter lacking any positive determination. This would seem to correspond to the view that God can make anyone a prophet. And, Kaplan continues, the view that the heavens will eventually pass away denies the possibility of a stable rational order.

I follow Kaplan in accepting P3 and P2 as Maimonides' own positions. I also accept the association between P2 and C3. But there are reasons for questioning the association between P1 and C2. Although Maimonides does not prefer the Platonic theory of creation, he allows one to hold it as an acceptable alternative. Nothing like this is the case for P1, the view of the multitude. What is more, Plato's theory does not completely deny the existence of a stable rational order. It maintains that we have such an order now, but owing to an inviolable natural law – anything that is finite can contain only a finite amount of power – the heavens are subject to destruction. That is a long way from unqualified belief in miracles.

By contrast, Davidson argues that C1 corresponds to P1 because both the Mosaic view of creation and the multitude's view of prophecy regard the phenomenon in question as a miraculous emergence of something from nothing.[33] C2 corresponds to P3 because both represent compromises between a completely miraculous view and a completely naturalistic one. C3 corresponds to P2 because both espouse unqualified naturalism. Although he admits that the evidence is not entirely clear and might permit either an esotericist reading or a standard one, in Davidson's view the fact that Maimonides decides in favor of P3 shows that there is some reason to think he actually prefers C2. We saw, however, that C2 denies the eternity of the world *a parte ante* and commits Maimonides to an analogy between the human creation of artifacts and God's creation of the world.

---

[33] Davidson, "Maimonides' Secret Position," pp. 35–36.

According to Warren Harvey, C1 corresponds to P1, C2 to P2, and C3 to P3.[34] If he is right, when Maimonides speaks of "all who believe in the Law," he really means all of the multitude, or as Harvey puts it, all of the vulgar who believe in the Law. This is unlikely given the lengths to which Maimonides goes to clarify the Mosaic position and eliminate simplistic interpretations – for example, that creation takes place in time rather than being the origin of time. Nothing like this is the case when it comes to P1, which he rejects out of hand. Harvey goes on to claim that Maimonides is committed to C3 and P3, the two naturalistic alternatives. It is well known that Maimonides assumes the eternity of the world in arguing for the existence of God in Book Two, but as he tells the reader, and as Harvey has to admit, that assumption is hypothetical. Although Maimonides indicates that some rabbinic authorities believed in eternity *a parte ante*, this does not count for much given that some accepted the other positions as well and that Maimonides follows up this remark by saying that eternity *a parte ante* is not his own view.[35] As a final argument in defense of C3, Harvey resorts to the unity of will and wisdom in God, a position I have discussed several times.

Aside from individual objections that may be raised against these interpretations, there is the general question of how tight the connection between creation and prophecy is. The fact that no set of correspondences is compelling and that some are obviously forced suggests that Maimonides may not have intended a one-to-one linkup. Perhaps all he meant is that both sets of opinions sort themselves into three alternatives and make us decide between naturalism and belief in miracles. In both cases he rejects naturalism in its unqualified form but accepts it in a weakened version. Although he defends creation, he meets Aristotle half way by accepting the

---

[34] Harvey, "A Third Approach," pp. 71–74.
[35] GP 2.30, p. 349.

eternity of the world *a parte post.* Although he admits that God can withhold prophecy to someone who is suited for it, he agrees that when prophecy occurs, it is a naturalistic phenomenon. So there is more in common between Maimonides' treatment of these issues than the number three. But that still does not mean there must be a one-to-one connection between the various alternatives.

The fundamental question is still: what conclusion do Maimonides' arguments support? The answer is that every argument he gives supports C1, which he insists is a foundation of the Law. Because C1 implies belief in the possibility of miracles, it legitimates P3, which is also the position of the Law. Whereas the connection between C3 and P2 is obvious, there is no reason we have to propose a connection between C2 and P1 except to say that neither represents Maimonides' preferred view.

## V

There is no need to review the centuries of esoteric interpretation that go from Samuel ibn Tibbon to Leo Strauss to scholars of the present day.[36] The crux of the esotericist reading is that the Mosaic view of creation is a myth that appeals to the average worshipper because it allows people to retain their belief in a God who responds to prayer and performs miracles. Because shattering this myth would cause people to turn away from Judaism and disregard the Law, Maimonides, it is argued, pretends to accept the Mosaic view but secretly directs his more sophisticated readers in the direction of

---

[36] For the history of esoteric interpretation, see Aviezer Ravitzky, "Samuel ibn Tibbon and the Esoteric Character of the *Guide of the Perplexed,*" *AJS Review* 6 (1981): 87–123; and "The Secrets of the *Guide of the Perplexed*: Between the Thirteenth and Twentieth Centuries," in *Studies in Maimonides,* ed. Isadore Twersky, pp. 159–207. For a critique of those who thought Maimonides should have followed Averroes' understanding of existence rather than Avicenna's, see Altmann, "Essence and Existence," pp. 156–62. For a critique of Strauss, see Alfred Ivry, "Leo Strauss on Maimonides," in *Leo Strauss's Thought,* ed A. Udoff, pp. 75–91; and *SFDG,* pp. 177–88.

eternity.[37] We saw that the esoteric view of creation supports and is supported by a naturalistic interpretation of prophecy.

The fact is, however, that Maimonides was perfectly willing to shatter religious myths even when he knew the average worshipper might be offended. His attack on astrology is legendary. He questions whether many of the miracles in the Bible happened as described and says without hesitation that we should not expect the Messiah to perform them. Even in works intended for general audiences, he rejects the idea that life in the next world will involve physical pleasure. Although he recognizes the need for people to believe in a God who gets angry at sinners, he says quite clearly that this belief is justified on the basis of its social utility.[38] He also recognizes that, important as it is, social utility must eventually give way to truth. In the end, every person must come to see that God cannot feel emotion, so that the passages that say God is angry or merciful have to be reinterpreted.[39]

In general, Maimonides' position is that ignorance on these matters is deplorable and may prevent one from attaining eternal life. This is why those with reputations for learning should make every effort to instruct people who labor with error and confusion. If belief in creation is no better than belief in an angry God, why does he not say the same thing about it? On the contrary, why does he claim throughout the *Guide* that it is one of the foundations

---

[37] There is an obvious problem with the esotericist position. If Jewish Averroists after Maimonides were open about their commitment to eternity, why would he have felt the need to hide his? To this question, Albalag (*Sefer Tikkun ha-De 'ot*, p. 51) responds with three claims: (1) the literal meaning of Genesis supports belief in eternal creation; (2) unlike the *Guide*, which is a religious work, his work is not intended for a popular audience; and (3) times have changed, and the average worshipper is more willing to accept eternity. We have already dealt with (1) in Chapter 1, n. 53. As for (2), I argue later that Maimonides' discussion of creation was not intended for a public audience. Like Albalag, Maimonides warns that a person who finds the book difficult should put it down. (3) is questionable in its own right. Albalag defends it on the grounds that people have grown more receptive to the position of Epicurus.

[38] *GP* 3.28, p. 514.

[39] *GP* 1.35, p. 81.

of the Law? It is true that, according to the Talmud, creation is one of the issues that is not supposed to be discussed in public. But the *Guide* is not a public document; it is a letter written to an advanced student and "those like him."[40] Given the difficulty of the material discussed from 2.13 to 2.30, which assumes familiarity with Aristotle, Ptolemy, and Avicenna, public access to Maimonides' doctrine was and has always been limited.

As Davidson notes, a wily philosopher with esoteric beliefs might offer familiar arguments on behalf of a position he does not hold.[41] But why, he asks, should someone go to the trouble of devising new arguments if his convictions lie elsewhere? Similar questions can be raised in regard to Klein-Braslavy's claim that Maimonides could not decide between creation and eternity and recommended a skeptical *epoche*. We can imagine a situation like this if the arguments for each position are equally balanced. But nothing like this is the case for Maimonides. Although he cannot demonstrate that Aristotle is wrong, he spends a great deal of time showing that the arguments for eternity *a parte ante* are not persuasive. By contrast we saw that the arguments dealing with particularity are said to be close to a demonstration.[42] I suggest, therefore, that Maimonides' convictions are exactly as he states them, that his arguments for creation and eternity *a parte post* reveal the full power of his mind, and that if he had wanted to agree with Plato or Aristotle, he would have said so and interpreted the prophetic tradition accordingly.

[40] *GP* 1, Epistle, p. 4.
[41] Davidson, "Maimonides' Secret Position," p. 36.
[42] *GP* 2.19, p. 303.

# 7

## Aftermath and Conclusion

LET US RETURN TO THE POINT WHERE WE BEGAN. Although its grammatical structure is unclear, the first sentence of Genesis describes the world in a way that emphasizes its contingency. If God confers existence on things, their existence is not necessary. From a philosophic perspective, this means that existence cannot be taken for granted. Prior to any question about the structure of the world is the question of its origin: why is there a world at all?

The three answers Maimonides considers are as follows: (1) God created it by an act of will, (2) God imposed order on preexistent matter, and (3) God is the source of eternal emanation. All agree that matter is generated; the question is how. The theories of Plato and Aristotle assert the eternality of matter and seek to explain its generation by a causal process. The theory of Moses asserts that matter comes to be along with everything else and that the manner in which it comes to be is not a causal process as we normally understand it. For Maimonides, causality is a horizontal relation that implies resemblance. Because God does not resemble the world in any respect, a causal relation between them is ruled out. This is why Maimonides turns to will. His only other option was to turn to Platonic causation and adopt some form of the "prior to $F$, therefore not $F$" principle, but doing so would still raise questions of purpose and particularity.

By looking at the world as the object of God's will, Maimonides gains several advantages. First, he can invoke the idea that the will does not have to bring about a given effect right away but can will what it wants when it wants. Even though God is eternal, it does not follow that the world or its material component is eternal as well. Second, he can avoid the "one cause, one effect" principle and point out, as he does at $GP$ 2.22, that a single act of will can accomplish many different things. It is true that God's will can be viewed as a cause to the degree that it has the power to realize anything that is logically possible. We saw, however, that it is not the sort of cause that forces us to posit a resemblance between it and its effect. Unlike a natural cause, the will does not pass something of itself to the object willed: it simply desires that the object come to be.

Unless there were an alternative to natural causation, Maimonides would be faced with an irreconcilable dilemma, for having created the world, God would have something in common with it. If God had something in common with it, the basic premise of his negative theology would be broken. Common features would pave the way for predication by analogy and other doctrines that Maimonides clearly rejects. Although it may involve a degree of anthropomorphism to say that God *confers* existence on things, the idea is that no finite essence has the power to produce instances of itself, so that the only thing that can produce them is God.

Looked at this way, Maimonides' account of creation is not a concession to orthodoxy but a necessary consequence of well-established convictions. Another advantage is that he does not have to say that everything in the world can be understood by human reason. Because the world comes to be by an act of will, it is possible for it to contain features science cannot explain. This allows him to compare our position to Job's when the latter hears the voice from the whirlwind. Given the size of the world and the insignificance of our place in it, there are and always will be phenomena that cause perplexity. For those that do not, he can say that although God's will is not transparent, neither is it frivolous or arbitrary: some things can be grasped by human reason, some not. He can continue to say that will and wisdom are one in God even if from our perspective, there are things that fall more readily under one category and things that fall more readily under the other.[1]

I

From a philosophic perspective, Maimonides' most important descendants were Aquinas, Gersonides, and Crescas. Despite religious differences, Aquinas is closest to him in spirit because he accepts a creation that is both *ex nihilo* and *de novo*. What separates them is the way these things are known. For Aquinas creation *ex nihilo* is indubitable. Because all things other than God are not their own being, "everything, that in any way is, is from God."[2] Maimonides

---

[1] Cf. Alexander Altmann, "Essence and Existence," in *M*, p. 154: "It appears that on the whole Maimonides related essence to the Wisdom, and existence to the Will of God, although he is rather vague in his utterances on the subject. He sometimes speaks of God's wisdom as responsible for determinations which are rationally inexplicable (II, 19), sometimes of 'the will of God or his Wisdom' (III, 13), but it is clear that what he really means is Will, voluntary determination (cf. II, 19). In God there is, of course, no duality of Will and Wisdom. They are both identical with His essence (I, 69; III, 13). But the distinction is a valid one from the aspect of existing things."

[2] *ST* 1.44.1.

would agree because even the Platonic and Aristotelian accounts of creation affirm the eternal generation of matter. We saw, however, that the version of creation *ex nihilo* that he ascribes to Moses says more: that God created matter and form simultaneously. Both thinkers would admit that the simultaneous generation of form and matter is not demonstrable, because it is possible to argue that matter preceded the creation of the world or that it is generated by the activity of the heavenly intelligences.

In regard to creation *de novo*, Aquinas makes a passing reference to Maimonides' argument from particularity in *De Potentia Dei* but ignores it in the *Summa Theologiae*.[3] The reason for this may be Maimonides' admission that if science could find an explanation for what now seems baffling, he would interpret the Book of Genesis in accord with Aristotle. Aquinas is not willing to take that risk. For him, belief in creation *de novo* is not a matter of evaluating evidence but of faith.[4] Thus, no scientific result can confirm it or disprove it. The price he pays is that the only way he can defend creation *de novo* is to cite Scripture. Accordingly, he takes "in the beginning" to mean "in the beginning *of time.*"[5]

Although this is the traditional reading, and the one favored by Maimonides, it is not the only one. We saw that some rabbis speculated on the creation of worlds before this one. To someone who says that "In the beginning" is a figurative way of referring to eternal creation, Aquinas replies that although eternal creation is possible, the weight of religious authority is against it.[6] Maimonides' argument is stronger: not only is religious authority against it, so is the evidence of particularity. Despite the efforts of both thinkers to discredit eternal creation, people continued to believe it – as we will see when we get to Crescas.

[3] *De Potentia Dei* 3.17 (*OTW*, p. 51).
[4] *ST* 1.46.2.
[5] *ST* 1.46.3.
[6] *ST* 1.46.2, reply to objection 2.

Gersonides defends creation *de novo* but takes exception to the claim that it cannot be demonstrated. He therefore argues that there are three criteria for determining whether something has been created: (1) that it serves a purpose or exists for the sake of an end, (2) that it possesses properties that do not follow from its essence, (3) that it contributes to the goal-directed behavior of other things.[7] To use his own example, it is obvious that while the essence triangularity does not satisfy these conditions, a triangle made by a craftsman does. The next step is to argue, with Aristotle, that because the heavenly bodies exhibit regular behavior and satisfy these conditions, they cannot be the product of chance. More specifically, their motion is not only regular but the most perfect motion possible; their respective sizes, orbits, velocities, and ability to emit light do not follow from their essence; and they obviously enhance the quality of life for creatures on earth. In regard to the latter, Gersonides points out that because the motion of the heavenly bodies is not for the purpose of obtaining something necessary to themselves nor for fleeing something undesirable, it must be for the sake of something else: to contribute to the perfection of life on earth.[8] If, as Aristotle admits, nature does nothing in vain, and if the heavenly bodies are organized to perfect life on earth, they must be the product of an agent who acts for a purpose.

Strictly speaking, the argument is not complete. From the fact that the world was produced by an agent, it does not follow that it was created *de novo*. As Gersonides recognizes, there is still the possibility that it was generated by a process of continuous emanation. He replies that continuous emanation, in which the heavenly bodies are created, go out of existence, and get created again in the next instant (i.e., a process by which God both creates and sustains the world in every moment in time) involves a number of

---

[7] *WL* 6.1.6, pp. 239–42.
[8] *WL* 6.1.9.

absurdities – for example, the constant creation and destruction of the same things, that time is composed of instants, and that heavenly motion is not continuous.[9] On the basis of this argument, he concludes that the heavenly bodies were created *de novo*.

Although Maimonides agrees that the heavenly bodies were created for a purpose, he is skeptical about our ability to know what that purpose is and casts considerable doubt on the claim that everything was made for our benefit. To be sure, the Torah (Genesis 1:17–18) says the heavenly bodies were created "to give light upon the earth, and to rule over the day and over the night," but Maimonides argues (*GP* 3.13, p. 454) this is merely a fact about them, not a statement of their purpose. Even when dealing with plants and animals, he thinks the purpose of most species is hidden from us (ibid., p. 449). As we saw, our intellects are incapable of understanding the perfection of everything God has made or everything he has commanded. As long as this is true, belief in creation *de novo* cannot be demonstrated. The closest Maimonides comes to a demonstration is (2), which amounts to a claim of particularity. But even here he hesitates to say that eternal emanation is absurd.

The biggest difference between Maimonides and Gersonides concerns creation *ex nihilo*. The crux of Gersonides' objection to creation *ex nihilo* is that it violates the principle that the effect must resemble the cause:[10]

> In general, a form gives something *similar* to itself; thus, it gives the form, for all forms are objects of the intellect [i.e., incorporeal]. But would that I knew how a form can give corporeality.

We see in this passage a precursor to Spinoza's belief that because thought and extension have nothing in common, they cannot interact with one another. If this is correct, all of the views Maimonides

[9] *WL* 6.1.7, pp. 246–49.
[10] *WL* 6.1.17, p. 325.

discusses are mistaken because at some point each of them claims that a form or intellect is the cause of matter. Rigorous adherence to the similarity of cause to effect would imply either that God is material or that God is not the cause of the material component of the world. Spinoza took the first option, Gersonides the second.

According to Gersonides, although prime matter preexists creation, it has no definite shape or form. Unlike the receptacle before the action of the Demiurge, it is neither in motion nor at rest.[11] In that sense, it could be described as nothing. But insofar as it is the substratum from which the world was formed, it has to be something and serve as an explanatory principle. Although Gersonides admits that our knowledge of it is inexact, he concludes that there must have been enough of it around for the world to be fashioned from it and that in all likelihood there is still some left over.[12] Aside from the question of how something that lacks any positive determination can serve as an explanatory principle, there is the question of how anything can exist independently of God. For Maimonides God's existence is necessary and everything else has existence conferred upon it by God. Nothing exists as a separate entity in its own right. If it did, it would be uncaused and thus unintelligible.

Gersonides' reason for believing in an uncaused substratum takes us back to Aristotle. Like Aristotle, he believes that generation proceeds from something to something else.[13] If one were to ask from what prime matter proceeds, the answer is that it does

---

[11] For the denial of motion or rest, see *WL* 6.1.17, pp. 322–24.

[12] *WL* 6.1.18, pp. 336–37.

[13] *WL* 6.1.17, p. 325. Cf. Aristotle, *Metaphysics* 999b6–8: "But if there is nothing eternal, neither can there be a process of coming to be; for there must be something that comes to be, i.e., from which something comes to be, and the ultimate term in this series cannot have come to be, since the series has a limit and since nothing can come to be out of that which is not." For further explanation of this point, see Charles Touati, *La pensée philosophique et théologique de Gersonide*, pp. 213–16.

not proceed from anything because it is presupposed by the generation of everything else. This is why the creation of prime matter is thought to be absurd. For a Greek philosopher concerned with the structure of the world rather than its origin, this answer may be legitimate. We saw that both Plato and Aristotle take certain features of the world for granted and do not ask where they come from. But this approach is difficult to defend once the question of origin is raised and the idea of a common cause of all things has been advanced.

To the objection that the eternity of matter puts it on equal footing with God, Gersonides replies that eternity is not the same as divinity: from the fact that matter exists alongside God, it does not follow that it has the same rank as God.[14] True, but the question is not what rank matter has but why it exists in the first place. If God is responsible for its existence, we violate the principle of causal similarity. If God is not responsible, the only other option is to say that matter is responsible for its own existence. How can this be if it has no shape or form? Gersonides does not say.[15] He simply assumes that creation requires an agent and a patient so that preexistent matter is metaphysically necessary.

Gersonides' next argument is that if the world were created *ex nihilo*, prior to creation, there would have to be a vacuum into which the world is put.[16] If, as Aristotle maintained, a vacuum is impossible, creation *ex nihilo* is impossible as well. Because the world is finite and all parts of a vacuum are the same, we also face the question of why God put the world into one part of the vacuum

---

[14] *WL* 6.1.18, p. 338.

[15] Note Wolfson's remark (*SHPR*, Vol. 2, p. 491) that Gersonides' theory is an evasion of the problem it sought to address. On the other hand, it may be that Gersonides accepted the generation of prime matter in his commentary on Averroes' commentary on Aristotle's *Physics*. On this possibility, see Steven Harvey, "Did Gersonides Believe in the Absolute Generation of Prime Matter? (Heb.)," *Jerusalem Studies in Jewish Thought* 7 (1988): 307–18.

[16] This argument is derived from Aristotle, *De Caelo* 302a1–9.

rather than another. Moreover, if the universe occupies only a part of the vacuum, we face the prospect that other parts of it may be left over and surround the world. Although there are numerous ways one could respond to this argument, the most obvious one is that of Aquinas.[17] A vacuum implies more than emptiness but space into which a body could be present. If there is no time prior to creation, there is no place or space either.[18]

Gersonides' third argument is that prior to creation, the existence of the world must have been possible.[19] Possibility requires a substratum in which it inheres. Therefore, creation requires preexistent matter that is the recipient of God's activity. This corresponds to Maimonides' fourth argument for eternity derived from the nature of the world. We saw, however, that creation *ex nihilo* does not require something that receives God's activity and is changed by it.

It is clear that in each case, Gersonides assumes that the origin of the world is continuous with its present state. To Maimonides' contention that inferences from the present state of things to the past are illegitimate, Gersonides replies that Maimonides is right, up to a point.[20] When dealing with the particular features of a thing as it is now, extrapolation backward is unreliable, but, he continues, it is reliable when dealing with necessary features. Seymour Feldman illustrates this with the following example.[21] Maimonides argues

---

[17] *ST* 1.56.1., reply to objection 4. For further discussion of Aquinas' criticism, and analogous criticisms in Crescas and Abravanel, see Seymour Feldman, "Platonic Themes in Gersonides' Cosmology," in *Salo Wittmayer Baron Jubilee Volume*, Vol. 1, pp. 389–90. Feldman objects that if the void is defined as Aristotle does – that which is empty of body but could be the place of a body – it is natural to conclude that if the world was created *ex nihilo*, there had to be a void prior to creation. But surely emptiness presupposes space. Another way to see what is wrong with Gersonides' argument is to recognize that the "nothing" involved in creation *ex nihilo* does not refer to a void into which the world is put but to the fact that God alone is responsible for the existence of the world. Again creation is not a species of change.

[18] *ST* 1.46.1.4.

[19] *WL* 1.6.17, p. 327.

[20] *WL* 1.6.17, p. 328.

[21] *WL* p. 328, n. 20.

that from knowledge of a grown person, we cannot infer anything about reproduction or gestation. Suppose, however, that we forgot about particular features such as size and shape and concentrated on essential ones such as the need for food, water, and oxygen. Could we not infer that a fetus needs them, too? For Gersonides, the need for a substratum in generation is analogous to the need for food, water, and oxygen to support human life.

Feldman does a good job of pointing out the limitations of Maimonides' example. Because Maimonides compares an early stage of human life with a later stage, it is hardly surprising that we can find similarities: a fetus and an adult are governed by the same set of natural laws. Because God is not a natural object and creation does not take place in space or time, Maimonides claims that we should not think of it as a natural process at all. Rather than an early stage of the world's history, it is the point of origin. Thus, any analogy to the growth of a living organism will fail if pressed far enough.[22] The purpose of the analogy is to show that extrapolation backward is risky even when we are dealing with easy cases.

From Maimonides' perspective, any claim that nature abhors a vacuum or that generation presupposes a substratum begs the question. Although there is nothing in our experience that involves the creation of form and matter simultaneously, Maimonides can always point out that our experience is limited to finite causes that pertain to size, shape, color, speed, direction, and other natural properties. Because nothing in our experience involves the origin of experience in the most radical sense, we have no right to regard experience as the final arbiter of this question.

In many ways, Crescas' theory is the flip side of Gersonides': instead of creation from preexistent matter, we have creation *ex nihilo*; instead of creation *de novo*, eternity. The best way to understand

---

[22] For a similar critique of Maimonides' analogy, see Alfred Ivry, "Maimonides on Possibility," in *Mystics, Philosophers, and Politicians*, ed. J. Reinhartz and D. Swetschinski, pp. 77–78.

Crescas is to return to the idea that even Aristotelians like Alfarabi and Avicenna accept creation *ex nihilo* if that means that God is responsible for everything that is. Crescas accepts this and goes further: both matter and form proceed directly from God by way of emanation.[23] In keeping with the normal understanding of emanation, he does not think of creation as something that occurs in time or even something that marks the beginning of time. The question is how he can reconcile eternal creation with free will in God. We saw that while Maimonides admits that the Aristotelians may speak of God's willing the existence of the world, from his perspective, they have no right to do so. Freedom means the ability to will or not will. Because the world did not always exist, God was free to create it or not and to endow it with the particular features we observe or others.

For Crescas, this is not so: freedom simply means that it is possible for the agent to perform the act and that no external force compels the agent to do so. Thus, it is possible for an act to be free even though it is determined by the desire or motivation of the agent.[24] On this account, there is no reason free will in God requires a point when the world did not exist. Why can we not hold that the procession of the world from God is not compelled and that the world has always existed? After all, if God is responsible for everything, how could something external to God exert pressure?

Why can we not also hold that God's motive is pure so that the world comes to be because of God's desire to share existence with other things?[25] Because God's love is eternal, there is no reason why the world, which is the object of that love, should not be eternal as well. If God's love and power to act are not just eternal but absolute,

---

[23] *Or Ha-Shem* 3.1.5.

[24] Ibid. For further discussion of Crescas' compatibilism, see Seymour Feldman, "The Theory of Eternal Creation in Hasdai Crescas and Some of His Predecessors," *Viator* 11 (1980): 307–309; and Barry Kogan, "The Problem of Creation in Late Medieval Jewish Philosophy," in *A Straight Path*, ed. R. Link-Salinger, pp. 172–73.

[25] *Or Ha-Shem* 2.2.4.

it makes no sense to suppose that anything can limit God to creating the world at a particular point.[26] On the contrary, infinite power manifests itself in the form of a world with no temporal limits. Like Spinoza, Crescas rejects the idea that God surveys a range of alternatives and picks one at the moment of creation so that God wills only a small portion of what he understands. Everything God understands is willed; everything God wills is completely understood. As the product of both, the world is eternal yet produced for a purpose.

Overall, Crescas' strategy is to reason from the eternity of God to the eternity of the world. His view is complicated by a passage in which he claims that according to tradition, *bereshit* implies creation at a definite instant.[27] Rather than offer an interpretation of such a cryptic remark, I would like to take up the challenge that Crescas' arguments pose to Maimonides. Although the eternity of God's knowledge does not provide sufficient grounds for demonstrating the eternity of the world, Maimonides never denies that the eternity of the world is logically possible. His argument is that both religious authority and the available scientific evidence are against it. The issue at stake is how we understand divine freedom.

We saw that for Maimonides, lack of external constraint is a necessary condition for freedom but not a sufficient one. If the agent can only will what follows from its nature, it makes no difference whether the cause acting on the will is internal or external: the agent is not free and cannot act for a purpose.[28] Nor will it do to say that the existence of the world is possible. For God to be free in Maimonides' sense, the world must be both possible and possible not. If the world is eternal, it has to exist and cannot be possible

---

[26] *Or Ha-Shem* 2.3.1–2.

[27] *Or Ha-Shem* 3.1.5. Does this mean that Crescas envisioned the creation of an infinite number of fine worlds or the eternal creation of this one? Feldman ("The Theory," pp. 315–19) opts for the latter.

[28] *GP* 2.20, p. 314.

not. If it is not possible not, to say that God faced a decision in creating it is to play with words.

II

Wherever one's sympathies lie, there is one point on which Maimonides is certainly right: that he has not succeeded in demonstrating his position. As he points out (*GP* 1.31, p. 66), demonstration provides finality. Once a matter has been demonstrated, there is no tug-of-war between opposing parties and no refusal to accept it. Nothing like this is the case with creation before or after he wrote the *Guide*.

To understand why, recall that Maimonides' discussion of creation seeks to establish two things: (1) that it is possible that God created the world *de novo* and *ex nihilo* and (2) that based on observation of the world around us, creation *de novo* is a more plausible explanation than eternity. The first suffers from the fact that according to Maimonides, we cannot know what God is or how God acts; the second from the fact that our knowledge of the world is always subject to revision. Even if these problems could be avoided, creation would still be something of a mystery because it is not a causal connection and does not take place in space or time. We cannot represent it in visual terms or try to emulate it in our own actions. At bottom it is a unique act undertaken by a unique being. Whatever our grounds for saying that it occurred, we will never be in a position to say how. It follows that our understanding of creation will always be presumptive. The price Maimonides pays for such honesty is that one of the pillars on which monotheism rests is less than certain. This is what led Aquinas to say that belief in creation should not rest on the evaluation of arguments but be viewed as an article of faith.

More than anywhere else, this is the point where we would expect Maimonides to hide behind the veil of esotericism. Having stressed the importance of creation, he would be putting his readers in a precarious position by claiming that it cannot be known with certainty. Surely it would have been more prudent to claim that creation *can* be demonstrated and then produce arguments that fail to do so. The majority of worshippers would feel secure in their commitment to a central doctrine of the religion, whereas the educated few would recognize that certainty on this matter is beyond the scope of the human intellect. Again Maimonides does nothing of the sort. Instead of shielding his readers from doubts that may arise about what he has argued, he tells them several times that they have no choice but to live with those doubts.[29]

This is in sharp contrast to the tone he adopts in the *Mishneh Torah,* where there is no suggestion that the Law rests on a less than certain footing. The difference can be explained by saying that Maimonides recognized that some of the things he had taken for granted earlier may not be true and that the readers of the *Guide* could live with the fact that human knowledge is limited. This is why he refuses to say that Aristotle's position on creation is absurd even though many of those same readers would have wanted to hear it. This, then, is another case in which the duty to tell the truth takes precedence over the need to conceal it. Having defended his position to the best of his ability, he admits that the speculative nature of the subject prevents him from doing more.

Although Maimonides claims that Aristotle did not think he had demonstrated the eternity of the world, proponents of the Aristotelian tradition of which Maimonides speaks did think it. For them the structure of causality sets the bounds of intelligibility so

---

[29] See, for example, *GP* 1.32, p. 68, where he makes intellectual caution a religious ideal: "For if you stay your progress because of a dubious point; if you do not deceive yourself into believing that there is a demonstration with regard to matters that have not been demonstrated; if you do not hasten to reject and categorically to pronounce false any assertions whose contradictories have not been demonstrated; if, finally, you do not aspire to apprehend that which you are unable to apprehend – you will have achieved human perfection and attained the rank of Rabbi Akiva."

that creation *ex nihilo* in Maimonides' sense and the possibility of spontaneous action in God are both absurd. Aside from the various objections Maimonides offers to their arguments, there is the additional fact that their arguments are multiple: four proofs of eternity derived from the nature of the world and four derived from the nature of God. Why are so many proofs needed?

If any one constituted a demonstration, there would be no need to rely on others. Note that we do not find multiple arguments in Euclid: once a theorem is proved, the issue is closed. By contrast, the more arguments one offers, the greater is the doubt that any one is valid. If none is valid, the mode of argument is not demonstration but dialectic. In the *Topics*, Aristotle himself cites the eternity of the world as a classic example of a question that must be decided dialectically.[30] The fact that Maimonides admits he has not demonstrated his position is not a sign that he is secretly committed to something else but that his frequent claims of fallibility are meant to be taken seriously.[31] To the degree that they are, the necessity of one position and absurdity of the other are impossible to establish.

### III

To raise the question of origin is to raise the question of existence. From Maimonides' perspective, the question of existence is one of Judaism's great contributions to Western metaphysics: the fact that God chose to create the world, did not have to make that choice, and having made it could destroy the world in a second if he wanted. In short, the existence of everything other than God is contingent. Although Maimonides does not address the relation

---

[30] Aristotle, *Topics* 104b1–17.

[31] On this issue, see in particular *GP* 1.31: "Do not think that what we have said with regard to the insufficiency of the human intellect and its having a limit at which it stops is a statement made in order to conform to the Law."

between existence and essence as explicitly as Aquinas does, his arguments on behalf of creation push him in the direction of saying that existence does not function like other predicates. We saw that the act by which God confers it on things is not like the transference of heat, weight, size, or color to a recipient. Those can be explained by natural causation according to observed regularities; existence is different. If the act of conferring of existence is unique, the thing conferred is unique as well.

The closest Aristotle comes to existence in this sense is being as accident. We saw, however, that he has little interest in this subject and suggests that *existence* is a mere name. Because an accident is something that is true of a subject but not a part of its essence, Avicenna was on firm ground in saying that existence is an accident. The problem is that it does not function in the way other accidents do. As Averroes argued, it does not fit in any of the nine accidental categories mentioned by Aristotle. Kant maintained that it is not a real or determining predicate because it does not add anything to our conception of the subject. If I say that a car is red and has manual transmission and six cylinders, I change your conception of it by providing additional information; if I say that it exists, I simply posit something answering to that conception. In modern logic, this is reflected by the fact that existence is not designated by a predicate but by a quantifier.

Still, if existence is an accident, it is an indispensable one. Although substances are prior to accidents in the traditional nine categories and generally receive them from something else, it makes no sense to say that a substance is prior to its existence, for without existence, both substances and their accidents would be naught. If that were to happen, they would lack any ability to bring themselves into being, with the result that nothing but God would exist. In this way, substance presupposes something that is accidental to it. On what does this accident depend? Maimonides' answer is that it depends on a creating God, something that Aristotle's philosophy lacked. Finite substances are not self-sufficient but rely on God to bring them into existence and keep them there.

Although Avicenna introduced the distinction between existence and essence and saw that the former cannot be explained in terms of the latter, his understanding of creation was too thin to allow him to see the full implication of his insight. For Maimonides, existence is the root of contingency, which means that it is something that happens or appears or is found. In one sense, Aristotle was right: because science deals with necessity, it takes no notice of existence in this sense. But Maimonides showed that the world contains things that Aristotelian science cannot account for, things that are one way but could just as easily be another. What are we to do with them?

Rather than wait for an explanation that may never come, Maimonides proposes that we see in these things an important truth: the world does not present itself to us as the effect of a necessary and eternal cause but as the outcome of a free and benevolent will. Formally, to exist is to instantiate a concept or satisfy a description. In a deeper sense, to exist is to be part of the order that God chose to create. Although Gilson may be right in saying that all of this is implied by the opening lines of Genesis, many people other than Maimonides read the same lines and came to a different conclusion. Maimonides' contribution was to show how an insight taken from an obscure biblical verse could become the crux of an entire worldview. Although it is a worldview that cannot be established with certainty, it is one that continues to play a decisive role in Western philosophy.

# Bibliography

### WORKS OF MAIMONIDES

*Crisis and Leadership: Epistles of Maimonides.* Translated by A. Halkin; discussions by D. Hartman. Philadelphia: Jewish Publication Society of America, 1985.

*Dalālat al-Ḥā'irīn (Guide of the Perplexed).* Arabic text. Edited by I. Joel. Jerusalem: Junovitch, 1929.

*Le guide des égarés.* Translated by Salomon Munk. Paris: G.-P. Maisonneuve and Larose, 1981.

*Guide of the Perplexed.* Translated by Shlomo Pines. Chicago: University of Chicago Press, 1963.

*A Maimonides Reader.* Edited by Isadore Twersky. New York: Behrman House, 1972.

*Mishneh Torah (Code of Jewish Law).* Hebrew text. Edited by S. T. Rubenstein et al. Jerusalem: Mossad Harav Kook, 1967–73.

*Moreh Nevukhim (Guide of the Perplexed).* Arabic text and Hebrew translation by Joseph Kafih. Jerusalem: Mossad Harav Kook, 1972.

*Moreh Nevukhim (Guide of the Perplexed).* Hebrew translation by Samuel ibn Tibbon. New York: Om, 1946.

### OTHER PRIMARY SOURCES

Abravanel, Yizhak (Isaac). *New Heavens (Shamayim Ḥadashim).* Roedelheim: W. Heidenheim, 1828.

Albalag, Isaac. *Sefer Tikkun ha-De'ot.* Edited by Georges Vajda. Jerusalem: Israel Academy of Sciences and Humanities, 1973.

Al-Bitruji. *On the Principles of Astronomy.* Edited and translated by Bernard R. Goldstein. New Haven: Yale University Press, 1971.

# Bibliography

Alfarabi. *Al-Madīna (On the Perfect State).* English and Arabic. Translated with commentary by R. Walzer. Oxford: Clarendon Press, 1985.

Alghazali. *The Incoherence of the Philosophers.* Translated by Michael E. Marmura. Provo, UT.: Brigham Young University Press, 1997.

Aquinas, Thomas. *Commentary on the Metaphysics of Aristotle,* Vol. 2. Translated by J. P. Rowan. Chicago: Henry Regnery, 1961.

*On the Eternity of the World* in Aquinas, *On the eternity of the world [by] St. Thomas Aquinas, Siger of Brabant [and] St. Bonaventure.* Translated by C. Vollert, L. H. Kendzierski, and P. M. Byrne. Milwaukee: Marquette University Press, 1964.

*Summa Theologiae.* Translated by Anton C. Pegis. New York: Random House, 1945.

Augustine. *City of God.* Translated by G. G. Walsh et al. Garden City, N.Y.: Doubleday, 1958.

*On Free Will.* Translated by A. S. Benjamin and L. H. Hackstaff. Indianapolis: Bobbs-Merrill, 1964.

Averroes. *Ibn Rushd's Metaphysics: A Translation with Introduction of Ibn Rushd's Commentary on Aristotle's Metaphysics, Book Lam,* by C. Genequand. Leiden: E. J. Brill, 1984.

*Tahāfut Al-Tahāfut: The Incoherence of the Incoherence.* Translated by S. Van den Bergh. 1954. Reprint, London: Aris & Phillips, 1978.

Avicenna. *Al-Shifā'.* Edited by G. C. Anawati and S. Zayed. Cairo: Organization Générale des Imprimeries Gouvernementales, 1960.

*La Métaphisique du Shifa.* Translated by G. C. Anawati. Paris: Vrin, 1978–85.

Brand, Dennis J., trans. *Liber de Causis.* Milwaukee: Marquette University Press, 1984.

Crescas, Hasdai. *Or ha-Shem (The Light of the Lord).* Edited by S. Fisher. Jerusalem: Ramot, 1990.

Galen. *In Platonis Timaeum Commentarii Fragmenta.* Edited by H. O. Schröder. Berlin: Teubner, 1934.

Gersonides. *Wars of the Lord,* Vols. 1–3. Translated by Seymour Feldman. Philadelphia: Jewish Publication Society, 1984–99.

Ibn al-Nadīm. *The Fihrist, A Tenth Century Survey of Muslim Culture,* Vols. 1–2. Translated by B. Dodge. New York: Columbia University Press, 1970.

Ibn Ezra, Abraham. *Commentary on the Pentateuch.* Translated by H. N. Strickman and A. M. Silver. New York: Menorah, 1988.

Israeli, Isaac. *Works Translated into English.* Edited and translated by A. Altmann and S. M. Stern. 1958. Reprint, Westport, Conn.: Greenwood Press.

Leibniz, G. W. F. *Discourse on Metaphysics.* Translated by P. G. Lucas and L. Grint. Manchester: Manchester University Press, 1961.

*The Leibniz-Clarke Correspondence.* Edited by H. G. Alexander. Manchester: Manchester University Press, 1956.

Narboni, Moses. *Commentary on the Guide of the Perplexed.* Edited by J. Goldenthal. Vienna, n.p., 1852.

# Bibliography

Philo. *On Creation* in *Works: English and Greek*, Vol. 1. Translated by F. H. Colson
and G. H. Whitaker. Cambridge: Harvard University Press, 1958–68.
*On the Eternity of the World* in ibid., Vol. 9.

Philoponus. *Against Aristotle on the Eternity of the World.* Translated by C.
Wildberg. Ithaca: Cornell University Press, 1987.
*On the Eternity of the World (De Aeternitate Mundi Contra Proclum).* Edited by
H. Rabe. Leipzig: Teubner, 1899.

Plato. *Timaeus.* Edited and translated by D. J. Zeyl. Indianapolis: Hackett,
2000.

Plotinus. *The Enneads.* Translated by Stephen MacKenna. 1917–30. Reprint,
London: Faber and Faber, 1969.
*The Works of Plotinus (Plotini Opera).* Edited by P. Henry and H.-R. Schwyzer.
Oxford: Clarendon Press, 1964–82.

Proclus. *Commentary on Plato's Timaeus.* Edited by E. Diehl. Leipzig: Teubner,
1903–6. Reprint, Amsterdam: Hakkert, 1965.
*The Commentaries of Proclus on the Timaeus of Plato.* Translated by T. Taylor.
London: A. J. Valpy, 1820.
*De aeternitate mundi (On the Eternity of the World)* (in English and Greek).
Translated and edited by H. S. Lang and A. D. Macro. Berkeley: University
of California Press, 2001.

Rabbi Eliezer. *Chapters of Rabbi Eliezer (Pirke de-Rabbi Eliezer).* Translated by G.
Friedlander. 2d ed. New York: Hermon Press, 1965.

Saadia Gaon. *The Book of Beliefs and Opinions.* Translated by Samuel Rosenblatt.
1948. Reprint, New Haven: Yale University Press, 1976.

Simplicius. *On Aristotle's Physics.* Translated by R. McKirahan. Ithaca: Cornell
University Press, 2001.

Spinoza. *The Ethics and Selected Letters.* Translated by S. Shirley. Indianapolis:
Hackett, 1982.

## Anthologies

Armstrong, A. H., ed. *The Cambridge History of Later Greek and Early Medieval
Philosophy.* London: Cambridge University Press, 1967.

Buijs, Joseph, A., ed. *Maimonides.* Notre Dame: University of Notre Dame Press,
1988.

Burrell, David, and Bernard McGinn. *God and Creation.* Notre Dame: University
of Notre Dame Press, 1990.

Gerson, Lloyd P., ed. *The Cambridge Companion to Plotinus.* Cambridge:
Cambridge University Press, 1966.

Hyman, Arthur, and James J. Walsh, ed. *Philosophy in the Middle Ages,* 2d ed.
Indianapolis: Hackett, 1986.

Kraemer, Joel, ed. *Perspectives on Maimonides.* Oxford: Oxford University Press,
1991.

# Bibliography

Ormsby, Eric, ed. *Moses Maimonides and His Time.* Washington, D.C.: Catholic University of America Press, 1989.

Pines, Shlomo, and Yirmiyahu Yovel, eds. *Maimonides and Philosophy.* Dordrecht, The Netherlands: Martinus Nijoff, 1986.


## SECONDARY SOURCES

Altmann, Alexander. "Essence and Existence in Maimonides." *M,* 148–65.

"Maimonides on the Intellect and the Scope of Metaphysics." *Von der mittelalterlichen zur modernen Aufklärung.* Tübungen: Mohr, 1987.

"A Note on the Rabbinic Doctrine of Creation." *Studies in Religious Philosophy and Mysticism.* Ithaca: Cornell University Press, 1969, 128–39.

Armstrong, A. H. *Plotinus: A Volume of Selections.* London: Allen & Unwin, 1953.

Baltes, Matthias. *Die Weltentstehung des Platonischen Timaios nach den antiken Interpreten.* Vols. 1–2. Leiden: E. J. Brill, 1976–8.

Barker, P., and B. R. Goldstein. "Realism and Instrumentalism in Sixteenth Century Astronomy: A Reappraisal." *Perspectives on Science* 6/3: 232–58.

Bussanich, John. "Plotinus's Metaphysics of the One." *CCP,* 38–65.

Charlton, W. *Aristotle's Physics 1–2.* Oxford: Clarendon Press, 1970.

Cherniss, Harold. *Aristotle's Criticism of Plato and the Academy.* 1944. Reprint, New York: Russell & Russell, 1962.

Cornford, F. M. *Plato's Cosmology.* London: Routledge and Kegan Paul, 1957. Reprint, 1966.

Corrigan, Kevin. "Is There More Than One Generation of Matter in the Enneads?" *Phronesis* 21 (1986): 167–81.

D'Ancona Costa, Cristina. "Plotinus and Later Platonic Philosophers on the Causality of the First Principle." *CCP,* 356–85.

Davidson, Herbert. "The Active Intellect in the Cuzari and Hallevi's Theory of Causality." *Revue des Etudes Juives* 131 (1972): 351–57.

*Alfarabi, Avicenna, and Averroes on Intellect.* New York: Oxford University Press, 1992.

"Maimonides on Metaphysical Knowledge." *Maimonidean Studies* 3 (1992–93): 137–56.

"Maimonides' Secret Position on Creation." In *Studies in Medieval Jewish History and Literature,* edited by Isadore Twersky. Cambridge: Harvard University Press, 1979, 16–40.

"The Principle That a Finite Body Can Contain Only Finite Power." In *Studies in Jewish Religious and Intellectual History,* edited by S. Stein and R. Loewe. Tuscaloosa: University of Alabama Press, 1979, 75–92.

*Proofs for Eternity, Creation, and the Existence of God in Medieval Islamic and Jewish Philosophy.* New York: Oxford University Press, 1987.

Dicks, D. R. *Early Greek Astronomy to Aristotle.* Ithaca: Cornell University Press, 1970.

# Bibliography

Dillon, John M. *The Middle Platonists*. Ithaca: Cornell University Press, 1977.

Dodds, E. R. *Proclus: The Elements of Theology*. Oxford: Clarendon Press, 1933.

Druart, Therese-Anne. "Al-Farabi and Emanationism." In *Studies in Medieval Philosophy*, edited by John F. Wippel. Washington, D.C.: Catholic University of America Press, 1987, 23–43.

Duhem, Pierre. *To Save the Phenomena: An Essay on the Idea of Physical Theory from Plato to Galileo*, translated by E. Doland and C. Maschler. Chicago: University of Chicago Press, 1969.

Dunphy, William. "Maimonides and Aquinas on Creation: A Critique of Their Historians." In *Graceful Reason*, edited by Lloyd P. Gerson. Toronto: Pontifical Institute of Medieval Studies, 1983, 361–79.

"Maimonides' Not-So-Secret Position on Creation." In *Moses Maimonides and His Time*, edited by E. Ormsby, 151–72.

Efros, Israel. *Philosophical Terms in the Moreh Nevukim*. 1924. Reprint, New York: Arno Press, 1966.

Feldman, Seymour. "Abravanel on Maimonides' Critique of the Kalam." *MS* 1 (1990): 5–25.

"An Averroist Solution to a Maimonidean Perplexity." *MS* 4 (2000): 15–30.

"The End of the Universe in Medieval Jewish Philosophy." *AJS Review* 11 (1986): 53–77.

"'In the Beginning God Created': A Philosophical Midrash." In *God and Creation*, edited by David Burrell and Bernard McGinn, 3–26.

"Platonic Themes in Gersonides' Cosmology." *Salo Wittmayer Baron Jubilee Volume*, Vol. 1. New York: Columbia University Press, 1974.

"The Theory of Eternal Creation in Hasdai Crescas and Some of His Predecessors." *Viator* 2 (1980): 294–95.

Fox, Marvin. *Interpreting Maimonides*. Chicago: University of Chicago Press, 1990.

Frank, Philipp. *Philosophy of Science*. Englewood Cliffs, N.J.: Prentice-Hall, 1957.

Freudenthal, Gad. "'Instrumentalism' and 'Realism' as Categories in the History of Astronomy: Duhem vs. Popper, Maimonides vs. Gersonides." *Centaurus* 45 (2003): 96–117.

Friedman, Richard, E. *Commentary on the Torah*. San Francisco: Harper San Francisco, 2001.

Frutiger, P. *Les mythes de Platon*. Paris: F. Alcan, 1930.

Gerson, Llyod, P. "Plotinus' Metaphysics: Emanation or Creation?" *Review of Metaphysics* 46 (1993): 566–70.

Gilson, Etienne. *Being and Some Philosophers*. 2d ed. Toronto: Pontifical Institute of Medieval Studies, 1952.

*The Spirit of Medieval Philosophy*. Translated by A. H. C. Downes. 1936. Reprint, London: Sheed and Ward, 1950.

Goldstein, J. "The Origins of the Doctrine of Creation Ex Nihilo." *Journal of Jewish Studies* 35 (1984): 127–35.

# Bibliography

Goodman, Lenn. *Avicenna.* London: Routledge, 1992.

*God of Abraham.* Oxford: Oxford University Press, 1996.

"Three Meanings of the Idea of Creation." In *God and Creation,* edited by David Burrell and Bernard McGinn, 89–106.

Grant, Edward. *Planets, Stars, and Orbs: The Medieval Cosmos, 1200–1687.* New York: Cambridge University Press, 1994.

Hackforth, Richard. "Plato's Cosmogony." *Classical Quarterly* N.S. 9 (1959): 17–22.

Harvey, Steven. "Did Gersonides Believe in the Absolute Generation of Prime Matter?" (in Hebrew). *Jerusalem Studies in Jewish Thought* 7 (1988): 307–18.

Harvey, Warren Z. "A Third Approach to Maimonides' Cosmogony-Prophetology Puzzle." *M,* 71–90.

"Did Gersonides Believe in the Absolute Generation of Prime Matter? [Heb.]" *Jerusalem Studies in Jewish Thought* 7 (1988): 307–18.

"Why Maimonides Was Not a Mutakallim." *PM,* 105–14.

Husik, Isaac. *A History of Medieval Jewish Philosophy.* 1916. Reprint, New York: Antheneum, 1976.

Hyman, Arthur. "Demonstrative, Dialectical, and Sophistic Arguments in the Philosophy of Moses Maimonides." In *Moses Maimonides and His Time,* edited by E. Ormsby, 35–51.

"From What Is One and Simple Only What Is One and Simple Can Come to Be." In *Neoplatonism and Jewish Thought,* edited by L. Goodman. Albany, N.Y.: SUNY Press, 1992, 111–35.

"Maimonides on Causality." *MP,* 157–72.

"Maimonides on Creation and Emanation." In *Studies in Medieval Philosophy,* edited by J. F. Whippel. Washington, D.C.: Catholic University of America Press, 1988, 45–61.

Ivry, Alfred. "Leo Strauss on Maimonides." In *Leo Strauss's Thought,* edited by A. Udoff. Boulder, Colo.: Rienner, 1991, 75–91.

"Maimonides on Creation." In *Creation and the End of Days,* edited by S. Samuelson and D. Novak. Lanham, Md.: University Press of America, 1986, 185–213.

"Maimonides on Possibility." In *Mystics, Philosophers, and Politicians,* edited by Y. Reinharz and D. Swetschinski. Durham, N.C.: Duke University Press, 1982, 67–84.

"Providence, Divine Omniscience, and Possibility: The Case of Maimonides." In *Divine Omniscience and Omnipotence in Medieval Philosophy,* edited by T. Rudavsky. Dordrecht, The Netherlands: Reidel, 1985, 143–59.

Kahn, Charles H. "The Greek Verb 'To Be' and the Concept of Being." *Foundations of Language* 2 (1966): 245–65.

"Why Existence Does Not Emerge as a Distinct Concept in Greek Philosophy." In *Philosophies of Existence, Ancient and Medieval,* edited P. Morewedge. New York: Fordham University Press, 1982, 7–17.

# Bibliography

Kaplan, Lawrence. "Maimonides on the Miraculous Element in Prophecy." *Harvard Theological Review* 70 (1977): 233–56.

Kasher, Hannah. "Biblical Miracles and the Universality of Natural Laws: Maimonides' Three Methods of Harmonization." *Journal of Jewish Thought and Philosophy* 8 (1998): 25–52.

Kellner, Menachem. *Maimonides on the "Decline of the Generations" and the Nature of Rabbinic Authority.* Albany, N.Y.: SUNY Press, 1996.

"Maimonides on the Science of the *Mishneh Torah*: Provisional or Permanent?" *AJS Review* 18 (1993): 169–94.

"On the Status of Astronomy and Physics in Maimonides' *Mishneh Torah* and *Guide of the Perplexed.*" *British Journal for the History of Science* 24 (1991): 453–63.

Klein-Braslavy, Sara. "The Creation of the World and Maimonides' Interpretation of Gen. I-V." In *MP*, 65–71.

*Maimonides' Interpretation of the Story of Creation* (in Hebrew). 2d ed. Jerusalem: Reuben Mass Press, 1978.

"Maimonides' Interpretation of the Verb 'Bara' and the Creation of the World" (in Hebrew). *Da'at* 16 (1986): 39–55.

Kogan, Barry. "Averroes and the Theory of Emanation." *Medieval Studies* 43 (1981): 384–87.

"The Problem of Creation in Medieval Jewish Philosophy." In *A Straight Path*, edited by R. Link-Salinger. Washington, D.C.: Catholic University of America Press, 1987, 159–73.

Kraemer, Joel L. "Maimonides on the Philosophic Sciences in His Treatise on the Art of Logic." In *PM*, 77–104.

Kreisel, Howard, *Prophecy: The History of an Idea in Medieval Jewish Philosophy.* Dordrecht: Kluwer, 2001.

Langermann, Y. Tzvi. *The Jews and the Sciences in the Middle Ages.* Brookfield, Vt.: Ashgate/Variorum, 1999.

"The True Perplexity: The *Guide of the Perplexed*, Part II, Chapter 24." In *PM*, 159–74.

Malino, Jonathan W. "Aristotle on Eternity: Does Maimonides Have a Reply?" In *MP*, 52–64.

Marx, A. "Texts by and about Maimonides." *Jewish Quarterly Review* N.S. 25 (1934): 378–80.

Morewedge, Parviz. *The Metaphysics of Avicenna.* New York: Columbia University Press, 1973.

Nuriel, Abraham. "The Question of a Primordial or Created World in the Philosophy of Maimonides" (in Hebrew). *Tarbiz* 33 (1964): 372–87.

O'Brien, Denis. "Plotinus and the Gnostics on the Generation of Matter." In *Neoplatonism and Early Christian Thought*, edited by H. J. Blumenthal and R. A. Markus. London: Variorum, 1981, 108–23.

"Plotinus on Matter and Evil." *CCP*, 171–95.

*Plotinus on the Origin of Matter.* Naples: Bibliopolis, 1991.

# Bibliography

Owens, Joseph. *The Doctrine of Being in the Aristotelian Metaphysics*. 1951. Reprint, Toronto: Pontifical Institute for Medieval Studies, 1951.

Phillips, J. F. "Neoplatonic Exegeses of Plato's Cosmology." *Journal of the History of Philosophy* 35 (1997): 173–97.

Pines, Shlomo. "Translator's Introduction." In *GP*, lvii–cxxxiv.

Ravitzky, Aviezer. "The Question of a Created or Primordial World in the Philosophy of Maimonides" (in Hebrew). *Tarbiz* 35 (1966): 333–48.

"Samuel Ibn Tibbon and the Esoteric Character of the *Guide of the Perplexed*." *AJS Review* 6 (1981): 87–123.

"The Secrets of the *Guide of the Perplexed*: Between the Thirteenth and Twentieth Centuries." In *Studies in Maimonides*, edited by Isadore Twersky. Cambridge: Harvard University Press, 1990, 159–207.

"'To the Utmost of Human Capacity': Maimonides on the Days of the Messiah." In *PM*, 221–56.

Rist, John M. *Plotinus, The Road to Reality*. Cambridge: Cambridge University Press, 1967.

Rosenthal, F. "On Knowledge of Plato's Philosophy in the Islamic World." *Islamic Culture* 14 (1940): 384–422.

Ross, W. D. *Aristotle: Metaphysics*, Vols. 1–2. Oxford, Clarendon Press, 1924.

Rudavsky, Tamar. "Creation and Time in Maimonides and Gersonides." In *God and Creation*, edited by David Burrell and Bernard McGinn, 122–47.

*Time Matters: Time, Creation, and Cosmology in Medieval Jewish Philosophy*. Albany, N.Y.: SUNY Press, 2000.

Sabra, A. I. "The Andalusian Revolt against Ptolemaic Astronomy." In *Transformation and Tradition in the Sciences*, edited by Everett Mendelsohn. Cambridge: Cambridge University Press, 1984, 133–53.

Samuelson, Norbert. "Maimonides' Doctrine of Creation." *Harvard Theological Review* 84 (1991): 249–71.

*Judaism and the Doctrine of Creation*. Cambridge: Cambridge University Press, 1994.

Sarna, Nahum. *The JPS Torah Commentary: Genesis*. Philadelphia: Jewish Publication Society of America, 1989.

Schwarz, Michael. "Who Were Maimonides' Mutakallimun? Some Remarks on *Guide of the Perplexed* Part 1 Chapter 73." *MS* 2 (1991): 159–209; 3 (1992–3): 143–72.

Schwyzer, H. R., "Zu Plotins Deutung der sogenannten platonischen Materie." In *Zetesis. Festschrift E. de Strijcker*. Antwerp: De Nederlandsche Boeklandel, 1973, 266–80.

Seeskin, Kenneth. *Searching for a Distant God: The Legacy of Maimonides*. New York: Oxford University Press, 2000.

Sirat, Colette. *A History of Jewish Philosophy in the Middle Ages*. Cambridge: Cambridge University Press, 1985.

Sorabji, Richard. *Time, Creation, and the Continuum*. Ithaca: Cornell University Press, 1983.

# Bibliography

Josef Stern. "Maimonides' Demonstrations: Principles and Practice." *Medieval Philosophy and Theology* 10 (2001): 47–84.

"Maimonides on the Growth of Knowledge and Limitations of the Intellect." Forthcoming in *Maimonide: Traditions philosophiques et scientifiques médievales arabe, hébraique, latine,* edited by T. Levy.

Taylor, A. E. *A Commentary on Plato's Timaeus.* Oxford: Clarendon Press, 1928.

Touati, Charles. *La pensée philosophique et théologique de Gersonide.* Paris: Mouton, 1973.

Urbach, Ephraim. *The Sages.* Translated by I. Abrahams. Jerusalem: Magnes Press, 1979.

van Winden, J. C. M. *Calcidius on Matter, His Doctrine and Sources.* Leiden: E. J. Brill, 1959.

Vlastos, Gregory. "Creation in the *Timaeus:* Is It a Fiction?" *Studies in Plato's Metaphysics,* edited by R. E. Allen. London: Routledge and Kegan Paul, 1965, 401–19.

"The Disorderly Motion in the *Timaeus.*" In *Studies in Plato's Metaphysics,* edited by R. E. Allen. London: Routledge and Kegan Paul, 1965, 379–99.

Weinfeld, Moshe. "God the Creator in Gen. 1 and in the Prophecy of Second Isaiah" (in Hebrew). *Tarbiz* 37 (1968): 120–32.

Weiss, Roslyn. "Maimonides on the End of the World." In *MS* 3 (1992–93): 195–218.

Wilamowitz-Moellendorff, Ulrich von. *Platon,* Vols. 1–2. Berlin: Weidmann, 1959–62.

Winston, David. "The Book of Wisdom Theory of Cosmogony." *History of Religions* 11 (1971–72): 188–91.

*Philo of Alexandria.* New York: Paulist Press, 1981.

Wolfson, Harry Λ. *Philo,* Vols. 1–2. Cambridge: Harvard University Press, 1947.

*The Philosophy of the Kalam.* Cambridge: Harvard University Press, 1976.

*Studies in the History and Philosophy of Religion,* Vols. 1–2. Edited by I. Twersky and G. H. Williams. Cambridge: Harvard University Press, 1973–77.

Zeller, Eduard. *A History of Eclecticism in Greek Philosophy.* Translated by S. F. Alleyne. London: Longmans, Green, 1883.

*Plato and the Older Academy.* Translated by S. F. Alleyne and A. Goodwin. London: Longmans, Green, 1888.

# Index

# Index

# Index

# Index

# Index

# Index